E S S E N T I A L
MERCEDES
COUPÉS, CABRIOLETS & SALOONS 53-67

D1592919

ESSENTIAL
MERCEDES
COUPÉS, CABRIOLETS & SALOONS 53-67

'PONTON' AND 'FINTAIL' MODELS FROM 180D TO 300SE
• •
JAMES TAYLOR

Published 1997 by Bay View Books Ltd
The Red House, 25-26 Bridgeland Street,
Bideford, Devon EX39 2PZ, UK

© Copyright 1997 by Bay View Books Ltd

Edited by Mark Hughes
Typesetting and design by Chris Fayers & Sarah Ward

ISBN 1 901432 00 9
Printed in Spain

CONTENTS

GENESIS
6

PONTON SALOONS
11

PONTON COUPÉS AND CABRIOLETS
28

FINTAIL SALOONS
35

W111 AND W112 COUPÉS AND CABRIOLETS
51

COMPETITION
64

LIVING ON
71

APPENDIX
75

GENESIS

When Daimler-Benz introduced the new Mercedes 180 saloon in the summer of 1953, the car had been eagerly awaited for some time. It was the first really new model to come from the Stuttgart manufacturer since the end of the 1939-45 war, as all the Mercedes saloons built since the resumption of car manufacture in 1947 could trace their styling and engineering roots back to the company's 1930s models. Six years on, Daimler-Benz was already lagging behind other German manufacturers in the post-war race towards modernity. No Mercedes model had yet embraced the unitary construction which Opel had introduced to the German market as long ago as 1935, and none of them could boast modern full-width styling such as had been introduced on the Borgward Hansa 1500 in 1951.

So how exactly had this great name of the German motor industry found itself in such a position? Perhaps the main reason was that Daimler-Benz had been reduced to a mere shell of its former self at the end of the war; as a statement issued by the Board of Directors in 1945

Exotics began to appear in the early 1950s. The 220 cabriolet arrived in 1951, followed by a coupé derivative in 1954. They were the direct ancestors of the two-door Ponton models introduced in 1956.

famously put it, the company had by that date practically ceased to exist. As a major producer of aero engines, aircraft and other war *matériel*, it had been a high-priority target for Allied bombers. The damage to its Sindelfingen factory was estimated at 85%, and that to the nearby Untertürkheim plant in the suburbs of Stuttgart estimated at 70%. Worse, its factories were spread across three of the post-war Allied military occupation zones, with Sindelfingen, Untertürkheim and Mannheim under American control, Gaggenau isolated in the French sector, and Marienfelde in the Russian sector, where everything of value was taken from it in the name of war reparations. Other German manufacturers – most notably BMW – had also suffered terrible losses during the war, but the Daimler-Benz plight was perhaps the worst of all.

In the immediate post-war years, Mercedes resumed manufacture with utility vehicles based on its pre-war 170V saloon. Seen here are a van with the factory's own bodywork (in this case a diesel-powered 1951 model), and the first post-war car – the 170V, barely changed from its pre-war configuration – that followed into production. The diesel engine introduced for the 170D in 1949 was crucial to Mercedes' post-war revival, and by the early 1950s had helped make the company into world leaders in the diesel passenger car field.

Like other manufacturers, the company clawed its way back to normality over a period of years, starting by building what it could to meet the huge demand for vehicles of all kinds. In 1945, it was estimated that West Germany (the collective name for the sectors controlled by the British, French and Americans) was in urgent need of 9000 trucks, 5000 buses, 25,000 cars and 10,000 motorcycles in order to re-establish the basics of everyday life. The priorities were vehicles which facilitated trade, and Daimler-Benz got back into production during 1945 with 3-tonne trucks at its Mannheim plant (which had largely escaped from the bombing) and 5-tonners at Gaggenau. Much of the production tooling for the pre-war 170V saloons had survived the hostilities, and in June 1946 production began of ambulances, delivery vans and pick-up trucks based on the 170V chassis. The 170V saloons followed in May 1947, and then the Unimog special-purpose 4x4 vehicle announced in 1948 represented the start of something new.

The Daimler-Benz recovery was undoubtedly slow,

The 1951 220 (left) introduced the overhead camshaft 'six' whose basic design would last right through the period covered by this book; this car's styling evolved from that of the 170S, itself derived from the old 170V. Introduced a few months after the 200, the 300 (below) took Mercedes back into the luxury limousine field; early Ponton prototypes used very similar styling, scaled down to suit.

but 1948 proved to be the turning point. Considerable help of course came from outside the company, for 1948 was the year when the worthless Reichsmark currency was replaced by the new and stable Deutschmark, and it was also the year when the US Congress agreed to General George C. Marshall's plan for economic aid to Europe, under which West Germany eventually received $3.5 billion in reconstruction funds. Daimler-Benz president Wilhelm Haspel established new credit lines with the Deutsche Bank and embarked on a programme to renew all the company's factories. He made Sindelfingen the centre of car assembly, while Untertürkheim remained the engine plant and the other factories were variously allocated to truck and bus production. Perhaps most important of all, the money was now available for Daimler-Benz to go ahead with putting improved cars into production – but there was neither the money nor the time to develop radically new models. The new cars would have to be evolutions of the old.

Design work had been under way since 1947, and the first of the new cars appeared in March 1949. Known as the 170S, it was really an up-market derivative of the existing 170V, which remained in production. It featured coil-spring independent front suspension instead of the 170V's leaf-sprung type, a reworked 170V engine with larger bores and a new alloy cylinder head, and an adapted version of the body seen on the 1938 six-cylinder 230.

The entry-level 170V and the new 170S were joined in May 1949 by another new model. This was a diesel-engined version of the 170V and was badged as a 170D. At a time when the market for diesel cars was largely untapped (there had been no volume-production types except for Mercedes' own 260D of 1936), this looked like an extremely risky move, but in fact it proved to be the right thing at precisely the right time. In the struggling economic climate of late-1940s Germany, fuel economy mattered a great deal, and when customers discovered that the new 170D offered fuel consumption of 5.5 litres per 100km (40mpg) and better without unacceptable performance penalties, they flocked to buy it in droves. Within two years, the diesel car was actually out-selling its petrol-engined equivalent.

There was further significance, however, to the introduction of the 170D. Its cylinder block was basically that of the existing 170V petrol engine, and shared the same bore and stroke dimensions, but designer Heinz Hoffmann had fundamentally altered the engine's pre-war

Another exotic of the early 1950s was the hugely expensive 300S, seen here in roadster form. It shared its running gear with the 300 saloon and, like that car, was developed over the years to take the fuel-injected 3-litre engine that eventually, as an all-alloy derivative, went into the Fintail 300SE of 1961.

side-valve configuration by redesigning the valvetrain with pushrod-operated overhead valves. Side valves were clearly on the way out at Mercedes, and the next new car (introduced some two years later) would have an even more advanced valvetrain design.

That next new car was announced at the Frankfurt Motor Show in April 1951, and re-introduced six-cylinder engines to the Mercedes range. The car itself was once again simply an evolution of an existing design, and despite the imposing-sounding designation of 220, it was essentially a re-engined 170S with flush-fitting headlamps to give a more modern appearance. The engine, though, was enormously important – and it would be the basis of the smaller Mercedes six-cylinder engines for the next decade and a half. Known as the M180, it had a swept volume of 2195cc and was designed to make the 220 a high-performance *autobahn* cruiser. To that end, its designers had aimed for good breathing at high revs, and had achieved this by providing large-diameter valves and the over-square, short-stroke configuration which was best suited to sustained high speeds. They had also simplified the valvetrain by using a chain-driven overhead camshaft operating directly on the valves.

This was an advanced piece of design for 1951, and earned both Daimler-Benz and the 220 considerable admiration from customers and motor industry professionals alike. Even the bigger 3-litre six-cylinder engine which was announced a few months later for the prestigious new 300 saloon could not improve on the M180's basic specification, and once again featured a chain-driven overhead camshaft running in an alloy cylinder head on a cast-iron block. The major difference was that the 300's M186 engine was designed for smooth power delivery rather than high revs; it therefore had

seven main bearings instead of four, and it had a long-stroke under-square design which would not rev so freely. That did not prevent it from becoming the basis of the 300SL sports racers and the Gullwing production coupé – and that is another story – but the engine is relevant here because it was developed into the all-alloy M189 3-litre which appeared ten years later in the Fintail saloons and the cabriolets and coupés discussed in later chapters.

The 300 saloon has another special relevance to the post-war Mercedes story, in that it was the last new model to be designed with a separate chassis. Like the 170V, 170D and 170S, it had an X-braced chassis of oval tubes which could trace its ancestry back to the first 170Vs of 1936. This was perhaps suitable for an essentially conservative luxury saloon such as the 300 was meant to be, and in any case monocoque structures had not yet been developed to the point where they were suitable for such a large and heavy car. However, there was no doubt that the monocoque had arrived in the European motor industry and that it was the structure of the future. That Daimler-Benz was looking at alternatives to separate-chassis construction became obvious in 1952, when the 300SL sports racers appeared with their lightweight tubular space-frame construction. And by then, Stuttgart's design engineers had already started to look at a monocoque structure for the next generation of saloons.

At this point, it is worth looking briefly at why monocoque structures took so long to gain a foothold at Mercedes. The monocoque concept existed by 1931, when the Budd company of Detroit built a demonstration prototype; the 1934 Citroën 7CV Traction Avant was the first mass-production monocoque car; and other European makers soon followed suit, such as Opel in 1935 and Morris in 1938. Yet Daimler-Benz, a company which led the automotive world in so many other ways, did not even start looking seriously at monocoques until the beginning of the 1950s.

The reason is actually quite straightforward: the problem was cost. In the 1930s, Mercedes-Benz was by no means a volume manufacturer, even though it did build some models for the mass market, and it regularly offered a number of different body variations on the same chassis. This was easy enough to do with separate-chassis construction, but to design and tool up for an equal number of monocoque bodyshells, some of them destined to be sold in only penny numbers, would have been prohibitively expensive. Monocoque structures lend themselves best to volume-produced cars, where the tooling cost can be amortised over a long production run. These were not the sort of cars which Mercedes built in those days, and so Mercedes models stayed with separate bodies and chassis until the early 1950s.

There were probably several reasons why Daimler-Benz decided to go for unitary construction at that stage. Among them must have been the pressure of market forces – the knowledge that rival makers were using this more modern method of construction for their smaller and cheaper cars, and that it looked bad for the prestigious Mercedes to use old-fashioned construction methods. But it was also true that the Mercedes passenger car division was planning on a massive expansion in the early 1950s, and was aiming to make and sell more cars than it had ever done before. These increased production volumes would enable the higher first cost of monocoque bodyshells to be absorbed without difficulty.

The plan to increase production volumes was closely bound up with Daimler-Benz's need to repay as quickly as possible the investment made since 1948 in its rebuilt factories. While the German market was returning to normal more swiftly than most observers had expected – thanks mainly to the German 'economic miracle' initiated by the Marshall Plan loans – the number of cars which could be sold in Germany was pretty finite for the foreseeable future. If Daimler-Benz planned to go for larger sales volumes, it would have to find new places to sell its products beyond Germany's borders.

So it was that the new unitary saloons which arrived in 1953 were born into an era of expansion. That expansion was startling: Mercedes passenger car production in 1952 totalled a respectable 36,824, but by 1957 the figure had more than doubled, to 80,899, and by the end of the decade it had exceeded the 100,000 mark. From 30,846 employees in 1950, the company had expanded to 46,226 in 1955 and to 67,521 in 1960. From

1952, when Daimler-Benz signed an agreement with the Hoffmann Motor Company of New York for national distribution of its cars in the USA, transatlantic success became vitally important to the company and the cars began to reflect American as well as European tastes. Similarly, expansion of the car business into Africa and the Middle East on the back of the truck business injected new requirements into the design processes, and by the time the Fintail saloons came to replace the Ponton models in 1959 the cars were being designed not just for Germany but for international markets.

THE KEY ENGINEERS OF THE MERCEDES PASSENGER CAR DIVISION, 1953-67

There was a remarkable consistency in the key personnel of the Mercedes-Benz passenger car division throughout the period covered by this book. The individuals were as follows:

Chief Engineer
Professor Dr-Ing E.h. Fritz NALLINGER (to 1965)
Professor Dr-Ing Hans SCHERENBERG (from 1965)
Chief of Design
Dr-Ing Karl WILFERT
Chief of Research
Dr-Ing E.h. Rudolf UHLENHAUT

Dr-Ing Rudolf Uhlenhaut, Chief of Research

PONTON SALOONS

An early 180D stands in a typical south German setting. Identifying features of a four-cylinder model include high vents (with bright trim) either side of the radiator and indicators mounted near the windscreen pillars. This car has been fitted with a wing-mounted racing mirror of a type popular in Germany, in addition to the standard external rear-view mirror.

When Fritz Nallinger's design engineers started work in 1951 on the car which was destined to replace the 170 and 220 models as the staple saloon in the Mercedes-Benz range, the decision had already been taken that the car would use an all-new unitary (monocoque) bodyshell. The major costs of the new programme were therefore devoted to that. Engines and suspensions had both undergone recent work for the 170 and 220 models, and so Stuttgart decided not to invest heavily in new developments here but to carry over as much of the existing designs as was possible. Some changes would be inevitable, if only to ensure that existing components mated up satisfactorily with the all-new bodyshell, but these were not expected to consume a substantial proportion of the budget for the new car.

Even though the 170/220 replacement was thought of as a *single* new car, it became clear very early on that there would in fact be two closely related designs. It would be important to have a clear visual distinction between the more expensive and prestigious six-cylinder models and the four-cylinder cars, and in any case the shorter four-cylinder engines would not need engine bays as large as the six-cylinders would. So it was that work started on two designs, coded W120 for the short-bonnet four-cylinder car and W180 for the long-bonnet six-

Strong unitary construction of Ponton saloon has upper body with its passenger cell (designed and patented by Béla Barényi in 1951) welded to a stout platform structure. More than a quarter of a century after the Ponton models had gone out of production, Daimler-Benz crash-tested a 220S to demonstrate the properties of the crumple zone and passenger cell.

cylinder. The longer bonnets of the six-cylinder cars located the front axle 100mm (3.94in) further forwards, and the designers added an extra 70mm (2.75in) in the cabin area, matched by longer rear doors, to allow the rear passengers more legroom. The additional 170mm (nearly 7in) in the wheelbase made the six-cylinder cars not only bigger but also more imposing to look at than the four-cylinder models.

The structure

The principles of the two bodyshells were exactly the same. Instead of a chassis, there was a heavily reinforced floorpan, which derived its rigidity from the deep pressings of the transmission tunnel and from the closed box-section perimeter sills which were linked to the tunnel by ribbed steel sheet. Curved box-section extensions led forward from the front of the transmission tunnel to form chassis legs or supporting rails for the engine and front suspension, while similar extensions behind the rear bulkhead provided the supports for the boot floor and the rear axle. Inner wings at front and rear were part of the stressed monocoque structure, but outer wings were bolted on to the monocoque and were not load-bearing. To all this was welded the body structure of passenger compartment pillars and roof.

The biggest loads would obviously be borne by the front of the structure, where the engine was to be situated, and here the Mercedes engineers spread the loads by using a subframe bolted to the front chassis legs, and fitted rubber blocks on the mountings to minimise the transmission of road noise into the bodyshell. This subframe carried the engine, suspension and steering gear, and could be removed if necessary for major service work. It was a steel pressing which spanned the chassis

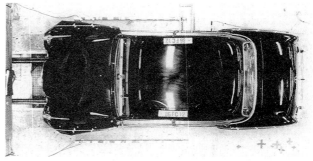

legs like a pontoon bridge (Ponton, in German), and this similarity led a German journalist to coin the name of Ponton to describe the cars. The name struck a chord, and in due course even Mercedes-Benz started to use it as a generic name for the cars.

This layout proved extremely successful and set the standard for large monocoque cars in Europe. It was quickly copied by other manufacturers, most notably perhaps Jaguar with their 1955 2.4-litre compact saloon and Rover with their 1958 3-litre model. However, its roots actually lay in the 1934 Citroën 7CV Traction Avant. As the Citroën had front-wheel drive, with the engine, front-mounted gearbox, front suspension and steering gear all co-located, its designers had put the whole 'power pack' into a detachable steel 'cradle' bolted to extension arms at the front of their car's monocoque bodyshell. Their principal idea was that the 'power pack' could then be easily detached for major servicing work, but a side benefit of the design was that the steel cradle also gave considerable extra strength to the front of the car. It was this aspect of the design which attracted the Mercedes engineers and, although the subframe of the Ponton models *could* be detached if major work was necessary, in practice it rarely was.

The feature which gave its name to the cars is the front subframe, which reminded one German journalist of a pontoon bridge spanning the engine bay. Note coil springs, anti-roll bar and finned brake drums on this late 220S subframe. For the first three years the basic petrol-engined four-cylinder 180 was powered by an old-fashioned side-valve unit developing only 52PS.

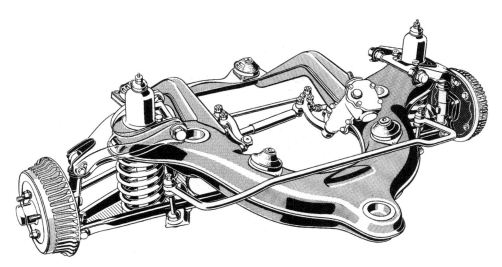

Running gear

The front suspension which that subframe carried was essentially unchanged from the type introduced on the 1949 170S, with twin unequal-length wishbones, coil springs and hydraulic telescopic dampers. However, the steering gear was new, with recirculating balls instead of the worm gear of the 170s and 220s – and it was criticised for being rather vague about the straight-ahead position. Mounting these items to a transverse subframe instead of to traditional chassis rails had presented no real engineering difficulties at all.

The rear suspension was also carried over from the older saloons, this time of course mounted directly to the monocoque. It consisted of swinging half-axles with a double pivot in the centre and a single coil-sprung trailing arm on each side, again with hydraulic telescopic dampers. Coil-spring independent rear suspension of any sort on a saloon car was advanced for the early 1950s, and it was the very fact that other manufacturers took so long to catch up which allowed Mercedes to retain the basic swing-axle design for another three decades.

However, as the performance of Mercedes cars increased, so the shortcomings of the design became more obvious. They were already apparent at the beginning of the Ponton era, when a sudden camber change of the rear wheels could cause an equally sudden and disastrous loss of grip in hard cornering. Work was in fact going ahead on improvements to the swing-axle design as the Pontons entered production, and a modified design was ready in time to be introduced on the six-cylinder cars which made their bow a few months after the first four-cylinders. This design, in which a single pivot replaced the double pivot of the earlier type, was also fitted to the four-cylinder cars after September 1955.

Engines and transmissions

As far as the engines were concerned, Mercedes planned to introduce their new saloons with the three existing 170 and 220 engines. So the W120 short-bonnet cars were designed around the M136 1767cc four-cylinder side-valve petrol and OM636 1767cc four-cylinder overhead-valve diesel, while the W180 long-bonnet cars were designed around the advanced M180 2195cc overhead-camshaft six-cylinder petrol engine. However, none of these engines remained unchanged from its previous incarnation in the 170-series cars. The four-cylinder diesel had tougher bearing material to improve durability and the four-cylinder petrol engine had a new carburettor, although its power and torque ratings were unchanged. The six-cylinder petrol engine, meanwhile,

Images from the original 1953 launch brochure for the 180. Cover view shows artist's licence typical of the time – the interior looks even roomier than in reality!

had increases of both power and torque resulting from a new light-alloy cylinder head, a different carburettor and pistons, a raised compression ratio and a 20% increase in the safe crankshaft speed.

Those engines drove through a revised version of the existing four-speed all-synchromesh gearbox, with altered second and third speed ratios. As the Ponton saloons weighed less than the separate-chassis models they replaced, Stuttgart's engineers had chosen taller overall gearing to improve fuel consumption at cruising speeds, and the internal gearbox ratios had been altered to maintain acceleration.

Styling

Buyers' expectations of styling had of course changed considerably since the 170V models had been designed in the mid-1930s, and even the revisions introduced for the 170S and 220 cars had dated very quickly. The extended

Images from the original 1953 launch brochure for the 180. Cover view shows artist's licence typical of the time – the interior looks even roomier than in reality! Individual front seats with fabric facings are shown, but a bench with rexine (plasticised fabric) trim could be specified to make the car a six-seater.

boots of the 1951 300 saloons brought their styling closer to the 'three-box' fashion which had originated in the USA and was now sweeping Europe, but slab-sided styling had now reached Germany. BMW was taking no risks with the swooping curves of its new 501 saloon, but Porsche's 1950 356 sports car and the 1951 Borgward

The first Pontons, like this 180D, had a tall and narrow radiator grille which recalled pre-war and immediate post-war practice. Despite its modest engine power, even the 180D was a big car, as the rear view demonstrates.

Hansa 1500 had employed 'envelope' styling – the Porsche to notably better effect – and new cars appearing in Britain (Ford, Rootes and BMC), France (Renault and Simca) and Italy (Fiat) were dispensing with the traditional bulbous wings, having slab sides in which the wings were suggested only by styling lines in the panels.

Karl Wilfert's stylists were not prepared to go that far – yet. The first prototypes of the four-cylinder Pontons looked very much like shrunken 300 limousines, with the same style of sweeping wing lines. However, there appears to have been a re-think some time in 1952, probably occasioned by the rash of slab-sided bodies which were

15

appearing in Europe. Daimler-Benz was counting on a long production run for its new saloons in order to amortise the cost of the new body tooling, and the company could therefore simply not afford to risk going into production with a style which would date quickly. The consequence was that the two Ponton bodyshells were restyled with slab sides, relieved by swage-lines in the panels to indicate both front and rear wings. At the same time, the sloping boot of the first prototypes was squared-up, to balance the bonnet in the 'three-box' idiom. Precise figures are not available, but there is no doubt that the changes brought with them more interior space; the boot of the production Pontons would in fact be some 75% more capacious than the boot of the 170S and 220!

The original 180

The first of the Ponton saloons to be introduced was the four-cylinder petrol model, which started coming off the assembly lines at Sindelfingen in July 1953 and was publicly unveiled at the Frankfurt Motor Show that autumn. It bore 180 badges, largely to distinguish it from variants of the 170 range with which it shared its engine and which remained in production for the time being. Pricing, at least on the home market, was carefully arranged so that the new car actually cost less than the 170S it replaced, and the 180 was received with huge enthusiasm. Sales in the first full year of production (1954) far exceeded the 170S models' best year (1950), and while the new car's success was undoubtedly helped by the healthier economic climate in Germany and by increased exports, there was no doubting the strength of its appeal.

The 180 was no performance car, though, and its high gearing meant that acceleration from the 52bhp engine in top gear was leisurely. Steering was vague about the straight-ahead position, and gear-changing was no picnic, either, thanks to the steering-column gearshift which was not widely liked. Column shifts, of course, were an American-inspired fashion, and Mercedes must have felt obliged to pander both to fashion and to the need to sell cars in the USA. The under-dash handbrake was also American in inspiration, and those used to a centrally-placed handbrake found it awkward to use.

The brakes as a whole were none too successful, in fact, because Mercedes' use of 13in wheels instead of the 15in types of the older cars had brought smaller-diameter brake drums. This had been done partly to reduce unsprung weight and therefore improve the ride, but

probably also because larger wheels would not have suited the new body styling. The latest design of twin-leading-shoe brakes on the front wheels did provide plenty of stopping power, but the smaller wheel discs did not allow heat to dissipate very quickly and the first 180s became notorious for brake fade.

Taxis and limousines: 180D and 220

Mercedes introduced the diesel four-cylinder Ponton and the petrol six-cylinder car together at the Geneva Motor Show in March 1954. They were badged as 180D and 220 respectively, although the six-cylinder car was often referred to as a 220a in order to distinguish it from the 1951 separate-chassis 220 which it replaced. That a six-cylinder Ponton was on the way must have been obvious to Mercedes buyers as soon as the 180 had appeared, and sales of the older six-cylinder 220 nose-dived as customers chose to wait for the new model.

Full production of the new 220 did not begin until June, and so the cars were not available through Mercedes showrooms until the beginning of the 1955 model year that autumn. Once again, they proved a stupendous success, and 1955 calendar-year sales were more than twice as numerous as the best sales year (1952) for the old 220. The new car was fast, too, and with a 150km/h (93.2mph) maximum and tall gearing, it was capable of making rapid and relaxed cross-country journeys, particularly on the *autobahns* of its native Germany. Handling inspired greater confidence than in the four-cylinder cars, thanks to the new single-pivot swing-axles.

This new rear suspension had been developed from an experimental system tested on a 300SL racer in 1952. Instead of having each swinging axle pivoted from a fixed differential (hence the 'double-pivot' description), it had the differential housing flexibly mounted to the body so that it could swing with the right-hand half of the axle. The left-hand half of the axle meanwhile swung from a single universally-jointed pivot low down on the other side of the differential. The new system reduced the camber change under cornering which had made the old one so unpredictable, and if it did not wholly eliminate the vices of the swing-axle layout, it certainly helped.

Mercedes had done a good job of distinguishing the 220 visually from the four-cylinder cars. Quite apart from the extra length, the car carried a whole lot more brightwork. There were stylish chrome indicator housings on the front wings instead of the purely functional indicator-cum-parking lights of the 180 and 180D (which always looked like an afterthought), and there

Detail views of an early 180D: dashboard shows clean and functional lines, and 'inset dial' style of speedometer found on four-cylinder models; power came from 1767cc four-cylinder indirect injection diesel engine with just 40PS; even the cheapest models had a clock, and this car also has period Becker Mexico radio and accessory flower vase so typical of the times; door has hard-wearing trim and ashtray; driver's side front wing is mounting point for retractable radio aerial, indicator unit and rear-view mirror.

were chrome rain gutters and window surrounds, a chrome strip running just below the windows, and another one around the rear wing styling line. Quarter-lights in each door window – fixed at the rear and swivelling at the front – also brought bright metal frames. There was more brightwork in the form of aluminium stoneguards at the leading edge of the rear wings, plus

twin bright strips running along each sill below the doors. Bright metal wheel trims with slots around their outer edges covered the whole wheel centre, and the three-pointed star emblem in their centres was bigger than the four-cylinder type.

Front and rear details were different, too. On the four-cylinder cars, the front panel which incorporated the air intakes was bolted to the bodyshell and remained in place when the bonnet and grille were raised, but on the six-cylinders the bonnet panel incorporated the metalwork on either side of the grille. The six-cylinder cars' grille was also wider and more steeply raked, while the air intakes did not flank it but were relocated at the bottom of the bonnet panel, just above the bumper valance. There they were almost invisible behind the standard twin

Launched a year after the 180, the six-cylinder 220 had a developed version of the 1951 220's overhead camshaft engine (right) fitted into the 'pontoon' frame. A different instrument style (below) marks out the six-cylinder cars, but the interior remains rather basic – note rubber floor mats – on this early version compared with later six-cylinder 'Ponton' saloons. A mysterious scene from 1955 (bottom) shows rotund Alfred Neubauer, who masterminded Mercedes' all-conquering motor racing exploits that year, trying a 220 boot for size, watched by Karl Kling, one of his drivers.

foglamps, although these lamps did not prevent them from picking up dust and exhaust fumes – one of the 220's few major failings! Larger rear light clusters and a bigger chromed boot handle at the bottom of the lid further helped to distinguish the 220.

The 220s had interior differences, as well. These were immediately obvious on the dashboard, which had wood trim instead of the plain metal of the four-cylinder cars and featured a ribbon-type speedometer above four rectangular minor gauges instead of a large dial speedometer flanked by the minor gauges. Even the clock was different, being more obviously stylised although it was still in the centre of the dashboard. As on the four-cylinder cars, the standard seating layout was a pair of individual front seats with a three-seater bench at the rear. A bench front seat was a no-cost option, and reclining individual front seats could be had on all models at extra cost. Where the four-cylinder cars normally had wool-cloth or leathercloth upholstery, however, the six-cylinders usually had leather. Even the six-cylinder cars had hard-wearing heavy rubber matting on the floor, however; carpets simply did not figure in the Mercedes saloon range at this stage. And the 220 brought with it an unexpected but hidden technological advance: it was the first petrol-engined Mercedes to have a 12-volt electrical system, instead of the older 6-volt type.

While the 220 was aimed at the successful businessman, the new 180D was pitched at a completely

All six-cylinder Ponton saloons have a longer nose with straked indicator housings and simple low-set air intakes either side of the radiator, but there are detail differences between these three models: early single-carburettor 220 (top), complete with fashionable white-wall tyres, has a chrome strip on the rear wing; later twin-carburettor 220S (centre) also has chrome strips on the front wing and door; 'entry-level' 219 (bottom) differs more substantially in mating the long nose to the shorter four-cylinder cabin (note the absence of a quarter-light in the shorter rear door) and having less bright trim (no wing strips, only one sill strip and no wheel embellishers). The latter pair of cars shared the same number plate for publicity photography...

different market. There certainly were private buyers who had been impressed by earlier diesel Mercedes and were keen to buy the new diesel, but where the 180D quickly found its niche was as a taxi. It was ideal for the job, with spacious five- or optionally six-seater bodywork, a huge boot, an economical diesel engine and immensely robust construction. That last characteristic particularly helped sales in the under-developed countries of Africa and the Middle East, and it was on the success of the 180D that the modern reputation of the Mercedes diesel taxi was founded. So well did the 180D catch on that its sales in the first full year accounted for 44% of the *total* number of cars sold by Mercedes-Benz.

Visually, the 180D was identical to the petrol-engined 180 except for its badging. It was audibly very different, however. Outside the car, there was no mistaking which

engine was under the bonnet, and despite Mercedes' best efforts, the deep thrum of the indirect-injection diesel intruded into the passenger cabin at all speeds. Speed was another area where the two cars had marked differences. The 180D's maximum was just 112km/h (69.5mph) as compared to the 126km/h (78.3mph) of the petrol car. It was also quite painfully slow to get under way, taking 39secs to reach 100km/h (62mph) from rest as compared to the petrol 180's 31secs. Nevertheless, its outstanding fuel economy and durability earned it a special place in the hearts of users all over the world.

The 1957 models: 190, 219 and 220S

With the 180, 180D and 220 successfully launched, Mercedes began to look at expanding the range further. Meanwhile, all three existing models were modified for the 1956 season. From September 1955, the two four-cylinder cars took on the single-pivot swing-axles introduced the previous year on the 220. The diesel engine's safe speed was raised (by altering the governor settings) to give an extra 3bhp, an extra 3km/h (1.8mph) and a 37sec 0–100km/h (0–62mph) acceleration time. And the 1956-model 220s had bigger batteries and improved brakes, now with Alfin iron-aluminium drums at the front and an ATE vacuum servo as standard (a servo had also been fitted to some of the final 1955 cars).

Customer response to the existing three models was one factor behind development of new types, but another was the arrival of keen competition. In particular, the six-cylinder Opel Kapitän was offering performance almost as good as the 220's while undercutting it significantly on price. So Mercedes resolved to offer a cheaper six-cylinder car with the performance of the existing 220, and to introduce a new top model with even higher performance. As a result, the original 220 went out of production in April 1956 and was replaced by the cheaper 219 and the more expensive 220S. Meanwhile, it was clear that customers would also be receptive to a more expensive and better-equipped four-cylinder car, and so the 190 was developed. All three new models went on sale for 1957, alongside the existing 180 and 180D.

Probably least changed from the familiar models was the 220S. What Stuttgart had done was to raise the compression ratio of its six-cylinder engine and fit twin carburettors to improve the performance. The 220S cut the 220's 0–100km/h (0–62mph) time of 19secs down to 17secs, and put maximum speed up to 160km/h (99.4mph). The only mass-produced European saloon which could out-perform it was an overdrive-equipped Jaguar MkVII with an engine 50% larger in swept volume. Jaguar's mass-production, of course, was not on the same scale as that at Sindelfingen, and so it was the German car which went on to set the standards for big saloons world-wide in the mid-1950s.

To distinguish 220S from 220, Mercedes had done nothing more than add a bright trim strip along the front wing styling line and fit 220S badges. The new car did have fatter tyres to match its higher performance, however, and a brake servo as standard. It could be bought in a range of two-tone paint finishes typical of the time as well as the single-tone colours which had been available on the 220, and equipment levels had been slightly enhanced, with a headlamp flasher as standard and a foldaway rear seat armrest as an optional extra.

To create the new four-cylinder car, Stuttgart's engineers had taken the W120 bodyshell and simply dropped into it a detuned version of the 1897cc overhead-camshaft engine introduced during 1955 in the 190SL sports car. The engine was really a four-cylinder, short-stroke edition of the overhead-camshaft six-cylinder type seen in the big 300 limousine, and in fact shared a number of components with it. In the 190SL, it came with twin Solex carburettors and 105bhp; for its 190 saloon application, it had a single Solex carburettor and just 75bhp, which was still usefully more than the 52bhp of the 180 and gave the 190 very much better performance as well as better fuel economy. This engine

Period publicity shots of twin-carburettor 220S models emphasise travel and export: the Middle East was becoming an important market for Mercedes, and remains so; sign to Berlin, detached from West Germany post-war, implies long-distance driving for this father and son; strong under-structure revealed as a car is hoisted into a ship's hold.

transplant turned the car into a W121 – confusingly, the same code as was used for the very different 190SL – but the bodywork was also altered slightly to help distinguish the car from the cheaper 180.

A broader radiator grille made the 190 look less upright from the front than the 180, and the impression of width was increased by horizontal strips of bright metal on the air intake vents which flanked the grille. The W121 shell also took on some of the six-cylinder cars' features, with swivelling front quarter-lights, bright metal rain gutters and a bright trim strip below the windows. Larger tail-light units, big chromed housings for the number-plate lamps, and a 190 badge, made the car distinctive from the rear, while equipment levels were also higher than on the 180. In an astute move to promote sales, Mercedes introduced the new model to the German market at the same price as the old 180, dropping the price of that model to make it more attractive and

cheapening its specification (for example, by replacing the original laminated windscreen with a toughened-glass type). The result was another success, as 190 sales climbed rapidly to make it a bigger seller than the 180.

Creating the third new model for 1957, the 219, was a rather more complex business because it involved the production of another new bodyshell. This time, the new shell was known by the code of W105, and it was created by grafting the long nose of the six-cylinder W180 shell onto the short body of the W120 four-cylinder. What Stuttgart wanted was a cheaper six-cylinder car. As the six-cylinder engine could not be fitted into the short four-cylinder engine bay, and as deleting chrome and various items of equipment would not make the six-cylinder shell look sufficiently different from its 220S incarnation, this curious hybrid was the chosen solution!

The car's hybrid nature was reflected in its decoration, too. It shared its limited brightwork with the new 190, although the front wings bore the stylised chrome indicator housings used on all the six-cylinder cars. Its engine was the old 220 unit, in exactly the same state of tune with a single Solex carburettor, and as the car was all of 20kg (44lb) lighter when unladen, it accelerated rather faster. Factory figures nevertheless suggest that its maximum speed was slightly lower than the 220's, which is rather hard to believe!

Whether the 219 ever justified the investment in engineering and new tooling which went into it must be debatable. Annual totals never attained the levels of the old 220 in its heyday, and nor did they match those of the 190 or 220S, the models above it and below it in the

Mercedes range. Nevertheless, the length of the car's production run ensured that it ultimately outsold the old 220 which it had replaced.

The 1958 models: restyled 180s and the Hydrak clutch

Just as the Ponton 220a had never worn its a-suffix on its badges, so the 180a and 180Da which were introduced in September 1957 for the 1958 season did not carry their new suffix letters. Yet they were easy enough to distinguish from the earlier 180s, because they had taken on elements of the 190 styling. That meant the new broad grille, larger rear lamp clusters, and number plate lamps in the rear overriders. From April 1958, in a late revision to the range, the 180 and 180D were also equipped with 190-style front quarter-lights. However, the 190 always remained visually distinctive, because the 180 and 180D never took on the more expensive car's enlarged wheel trims or the bright trim it carried on the air intakes flanking the grille.

It was the restyle which earned the cars that suffix letter, but arguably the most important revision for the 1958 season affected only the petrol-engined 180. Out went the old 52PS side-valve engine, and in its place arrived a detuned version of the 190's larger-capacity four-cylinder. A single-choke carburettor replaced the 190's compound-choke type, and the compression ratio was lowered a few points. The result was a 65PS engine which gave the 180 performance which Mercedes needed no longer to be ashamed of – and the fact that it had a modern overhead-camshaft layout instead of the outmoded side-valve configuration made its own

important contribution to the Mercedes image of advanced technology.

The two six-cylinder models – 219 and 220S – were also revised for the 1958 season. The quality of petrol world-wide was now stabilising, and so Mercedes was able to raise compression ratios without the risk of engine damage through detonation caused by poor quality fuel. Higher compression ratios took the 85PS single-carburettor engine up to 90PS for the 219, and the 100PS twin-carburettor 220S engine up to 106PS. The 219 was further modified with a higher rear axle ratio of 3.9:1 to improve its fuel economy, while different ratios for the intermediate gears ensured that acceleration was not harmed. Both six-cylinder models were also given uprated rear dampers, and both could be bought with the new option of the Hydrak clutch.

The Hydrak clutch turned out to be one of Mercedes' less successful experiments with new technology, although it certainly seemed like a good idea at the time. In the later 1950s, many European car makers were experimenting with alternatives to the traditional manual gearbox, because they wanted to offer the simplicity of the automatic gearboxes which were sweeping the American market. Automatic transmissions were still great squanderers of power, however, and were therefore suitable only for large-engined cars such as were common in the USA; in Europe, automatics were found only on big saloons like the Jaguar (3.4 litres), the Rolls-Royce (4.9 litres), and Mercedes' own 300, which could be ordered with an optional three-speed automatic behind its 3-litre engine from 1955. In Germany, component manufacturer Fichtel und Sachs developed the Hydrak automatic clutch, and Mercedes adopted it.

A new overhead camshaft engine (right) was introduced to the four-cylinder Pontons with the 190 in 1956; this M121 engine, which displaced 1897cc and promised 75PS, had been seen earlier in 105PS twin-carburettor form in the 190SL sports car. The following year the Hydrak automatic clutch (below) was an innovative option for the six-cylinder models, but did not prove popular.

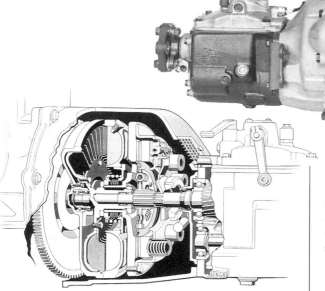

One advantage of the Hydrak was that it could be used with the standard four-speed manual gearbox. What it did was to actuate the clutch automatically as the driver moved the gear lever, thus combining two-pedal control with a manual gearshift. Pressure on the gear lever operated a vacuum servo which disengaged and re-engaged the clutch, and gearchanges were cushioned by a torque converter in the driveline. An additional refinement was a switch on the flexibly-mounted final drive which controlled the rate of the clutch's engagement according to whether the car was accelerating (when the final drive moved rearwards) or decelerating (when it moved forwards). There was also a reversed freewheel in the driveline, which locked up on the overrun to give engine braking.

In practice, the Hydrak worked well; the problems lay with drivers who misused it. If a driver treated it like a fully automatic transmission and did not lift his foot off the accelerator pedal when changing gear, gearchanges would be rough and the clutch plate would wear quickly.

Similarly, if he left his hand on the gear lever, he stood a good chance of inadvertently disengaging the clutch, a manoeuvre which had an interest all its own! So the Hydrak never became a very popular option on the six-cylinder Pontons, and Mercedes did not include it in the specification of the Fintail cars which replaced them in 1959, preferring to develop an in-house automatic.

There were also other revisions which affected the whole of the Ponton range for 1958. Probably most obvious was the introduction of a factory-fitted fabric sunroof as an extra-cost option on all the Ponton saloons, while there were also brighter interior colours and more supportive seats. The dashboard-mounted 'octane selector' was also deleted from petrol-powered models; it had been essential while petrol quality had been variable in the early 1950s, but now that quality had stabilised, Mercedes considered that a vernier adjustment on the distributor would cope with whatever problems arose.

New models for 1959: 190D and 220SE

At the Frankfurt Motor Show in September 1958, Mercedes announced two new additions to the Ponton saloon range. These were the 190D and 220SE, each in its own way designed to expand the range into more expensive territory.

World-wide sales of the 180D had increased every year since the model's introduction, and it was clear to

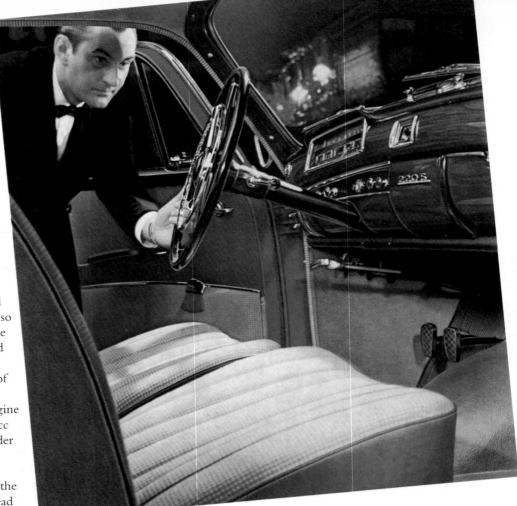

Mercedes that there was scope for a more expensive, better-equipped and better-performing diesel Ponton. What was needed was a diesel equivalent of the 190, positioned just above the 180D in the same way as the 190 stood above the petrol-engined 180. There was an obvious way forward, too: just as the 180's petrol engine had been developed into a diesel engine, so the 190's petrol engine could be developed into a diesel. And so it was, under the direction of the same Heinz Hoffmann who had developed the 1767cc diesel engine from the petrol engine of the same capacity.

The new OM621 diesel engine therefore shared the same 1897cc swept volume as the four-cylinder petrol engine in the 190. It also shared that engine's overhead-camshaft layout, but in place of the petrol engine's alloy cylinder head came a more robust cast-iron type which incorporated the pre-chambers of the indirect-injection diesel engine. The OM621 was not enormously more powerful than the smaller-capacity OM636, but it was noticeably smoother and quieter, and the extra 9PS improved the maximum speed while a little extra torque slightly higher up the rev range helped acceleration. Mercedes also took the opportunity of the new engine's introduction to give the 190D better starting arrangements than the older diesel car had, with the glow-plugs being activated by the ignition key rather than by a separate switch.

In most other respects, the 190D was identical to the petrol-engined 190, although it had the ordinary drum brakes of the 180D rather than the 190's finned type. Visually, it was identical to the 190 except for its badging – but the original 190D lasted for only one season, because the 1960-model cars picked up a number of modifications.

The new 220SE lasted only one season, too, although in this case it was because the car was directly replaced in September 1959 by a Fintail model bearing the same designation. For this reason – and because it was always

intended to be a high-priced, low-volume model – the 220SE became the rarest of all the Ponton saloons. Fewer than 2000 were built in the 12 months it was on sale.

With the 220SE, Mercedes brought fuel injection to its medium-sized saloon range for the first time. The company had already pioneered fuel injection during 1954 with the 300SL Gullwing sports coupé; a year later, fuel injection was introduced on the vastly expensive 300S coupé, roadster and cabriolet models to turn them into 300Sc types; Mercedes remained the only car maker in the world to offer fuel injection until General Motors in America introduced it on the 1957-model Corvette.

The fuel injection technology used by Mercedes-Benz had been developed by the German Bosch company, and could trace its origins back to systems designed for World War II fighter planes. The 3-litre engines had boasted a complex and expensive set-up with individual fuel metering for each of their six cylinders, but for the 220SE a cheaper and simpler system was employed. This had a twin-plunger injection pump which delivered fuel to fixed calibrated injectors, which drew air from a collector chamber; it also had some refinements to improve fuel

Furnishings in the 220S were of the highest standard: wood is the theme for dashboard and windscreen surround, while carpeted floor and fabric seating give added comfort. Rear legroom looks so good because the front seats have been removed for this brochure shot!

some time been distributed by the Studebaker-Packard Corporation across the Atlantic (the company would not establish its own North American operation until 1962), and feedback from that organisation made clear that the 300SL and the Chevrolet Corvette had persuaded Americans to associate fuel injection with high performance. So Mercedes equipped the 220SEs for the US market with a special gearbox which had lower indirect ratios in order to improve off-the-line acceleration. Relatively few such cars were built, however, not least because the 220SE was an expensive and individualistic purchase in the USA.

consumption and starting performance, notably an overrun fuel shut-off and an outside temperature monitor which controlled the amount of fuel delivered. By the standards of later electronic injection systems, this mechanical injection was crude – but for 1958 it was very advanced indeed. It also worked, whereas the Rochester fuel injection used by Chevrolet proved to be notoriously troublesome in service.

The Bosch injection system was fitted to what was otherwise the same 2195cc engine as came in the other six-cylinder models. It did not offer much extra power – what Mercedes called the M127 gave 115PS as compared to the 106PS of the M180 engine in the 220S – but it did accelerate rather faster than the 220S and it was considerably more flexible as a result of increased torque. The 220SE was given its own model code of W128, although it was in practice identical to the W180 220S in all respects except that of its engine and fuel tank. The latter had a slightly reduced capacity, as a result of different pick-up arrangements for the injection system.

Flexibility may have been the main selling-point in Europe, but it was performance which was becoming increasingly important in the USA. Mercedes had for

1960: the b-suffix four-cylinders

When Mercedes introduced the new six-cylinder Fintail saloons at the Frankfurt Motor Show in September 1959, production of the six-cylinder Ponton saloons was halted. All three models – 219, 220S and 220SE – were replaced by new equivalents, although there would be no four-cylinder Fintails before 1961. In the intervening two years, revised Ponton four-cylinders therefore remained available. There were four of these, known internally as the 180b, 180Db, 190b and 190Db, although as usual the suffix letter was never reflected in the badging.

The main reasons for the changes were to prevent the cars looking too old-fashioned alongside the new Fintail six-cylinders. So the Ponton models' appearance was altered to emphasise the family resemblance between the two ranges: the lower bonnet line, broader radiator grille and fatter bumpers (without overriders) of the 1960-model Pontons all echoed their Fintail equivalents. At the back, larger rear lights helped to modernise the appearance, and now incorporated the red reflectors which on earlier Pontons had been slung beneath the overriders. The 180 and 180D were also fitted with the larger 190 style of wheel trims.

Equally striking were the interior changes. All four models were given new passive-safety features derived from those of the Fintails – a steering wheel with a padded boss, extra padding on the dashboard, and deformable plastic switchgear. With the new steering

Fuel injection moved from the high-priced exotics in the Mercedes range to the top end of the saloon range in 1958, for that year's 220SE. A sliding fabric sunroof could be specified from very early on.

wheel came a stalk control for the direction indicators, as the horn ring no longer doubled as the indicator control switch, and that stalk doubled as a headlamp flasher. A pedal-operated windscreen wash/wipe system was also standard, and the 180s and 180Ds laid claim to new upholstery and door trims.

There were a few other running modifications. A brake servo joined the options list for both petrol Pontons, and all four models had the finned front drums earlier fitted only to the 190s. This change was probably made mainly to simplify production, as it was certainly not justified by performance gains. The engines in the 180D and 190D remained unchanged, and although the petrol 180 gained 3PS (from a new carburettor) and the petrol 190 gained 5PS (from a higher compression ratio), the small improvements in top-end speed would not alone have justified the more powerful brakes.

Swan song: the c-suffix 180 and 180D (1962)

It was all-change in the Mercedes four-cylinder ranges at the 1961 Frankfurt Show, when the existing six-cylinder Fintails were joined by new four-cylinder derivatives. Yet the Mercedes policy was to push its products gradually further and further up market, and so the entry-level Fintails were 190s and 190Ds instead of the 180s and 180Ds of the Ponton range. However, Mercedes tried to avoid alienating customers of its cheaper cars by keeping the Ponton 180 and 180D in production for another year. Both models were modified slightly for this final season, but neither was replaced when production came to an end in 1962.

The 1962-season modifications were confined to the engines of the two cars, and both 180 and 180D looked identical to the models they superseded. These engine

These cars can be immediately distinguished as post-1959 (b-suffix) four-cylinder models: front (190D) shows lower bonnet line, larger bumpers and broader radiator grille; rear (180) shows larger lamp units and bumpers; interior (180D) has new steering wheel with central padding, reflecting Mercedes' increasing preoccupation with safety and taken from the new Fintail range.

modifications brought about a new suffix letter, and within the Mercedes-Benz organisation the cars were known as 180c and 180Dc types. A new valvetrain, camshaft and carburettor were the only distinguishing features of the 180c, but the 180D was completely re-engined with the latest 1988cc diesel engine. This was a large-bore edition of the previous 1897cc type and was also found in the new Fintail 190D, although the version fitted to the Ponton 180D was of course rather less powerful in order to maintain the differentials between the two models. It was nevertheless more powerful and offered better performance than the older 1897cc engine, and that kept the customers happy – so happy, in fact, that the 180D sold better in its final year than it had for the two which preceded it. Meanwhile, Mercedes salesmen were no doubt busy persuading these same customers that, for their next diesel Mercedes, they should consider upgrading to the new 190D.

Utility and commercial derivatives

From 1954 until the end of 180 and 180D production in 1962, Mercedes offered Ponton derivatives designed for utility and light commercial uses. However, although the floorpan, drivetrain, suspension and front panels of these derivatives were manufactured at Stuttgart, the main bodywork was constructed by specialist companies whose products were approved by Mercedes-Benz. Most of these bodies also incorporated other elements of the saloons, such as doors and windscreens.

The most numerous light commercial Ponton derivatives were the ambulances, which could be based on any of the four-cylinder models and on all the six-cylinder types except for the 220SE. There were two major types, one built by Binz, whose coachworks were at Lorch in Württemburg, and the other built by Christian Miesen in Bonn. Miesen was new to working with Mercedes-Benz, but the Binz firm had built estate-type bodies for Police work on the separate-chassis 170S and 220 from 1950.

Both ambulance designs were four-door types, with a third rear window on each side which enabled the same basic bodywork to be used for 'Kombi' (estate car) derivatives. The Miesen design was perhaps the more modern-looking, with a flatter roof line and squarer rear quarters; the Binz design had a more rounded back and roof, and looked rather taller.

The ambulance and estate car bodies were the only ones offered on the basis of the six-cylinder Pontons. Four-cylinder units were also supplied with either two or four doors for special bodywork to be fitted, and these special bodies included a number of hearses.

PONTON COUPÉS AND CABRIOLETS

Top up or down, the Ponton cabriolet was an elegant car, with exclusivity part of the appeal – limited production of coupés and cabriolets averaged only around 1000 examples a year between 1956-60.

The tradition of the glamorous Mercedes-Benz 'personal car' dates back to the 1930s and to cars like the supercharged 540K. Such cars were always intended to be produced in limited numbers and at high cost, to satisfy the demands of a wealthy clientele. From Stuttgart's point of view, their exclusivity also aroused wide interest and therefore provided excellent free publicity for the company. That these cars also carried the very latest in Mercedes-Benz engineering advances further helped to promote an image of the company as being at the forefront of new developments.

In the 1950s, the tradition of the glamorous and exclusive 'personal car' was carried on by the 300S models, hugely expensive hand-built cabriolets, roadsters and coupés available after 1951 on a shortened 300 limousine chassis. There should perhaps have been only one such model in the Mercedes range, but when it

This 1960 220SE coupé (with optional steel sliding sunroof) was sold in the USA, which took large numbers of these expensive cars. Lighting regulations there demanded smaller sealed-beam headlamps and additional lamps in the wing fronts, not seen on cars for other markets. From the rear, post-1959 cars can be distinguished by the position of the model designation on the left-hand side; previously it was below the central three-pointed star.

became clear that a roadgoing 300SL Gullwing coupé would find plenty of customers, the company followed the dictates of the market and introduced one in 1954. There was no real conflict between the two models: the rather grand 300S and the high-performance 300SL appealed to rather different types of customer, whose only common denominator may have been wealth.

Cars like these, however, were beyond the reach of most people. The basic cost of a 300S in the early 1950s was 34,500DM, an enormous sum which comes sharply into focus when compared with the 12,500DM of the

top-model 220 Ponton saloon of the time. The 300S had the image of a car built to order for crowned heads of state – not far off the truth. Yet Mercedes recognised that there was also a market for a rather less expensive but still exclusive 'personal car' mid-way between these two, and to that end the company built cabriolets and coupés on the chassis of the old 220 model in the first half of the 1950s. When the separate-chassis 220 saloon was replaced by the new Ponton 220, it was clear that there would have to be new cabriolets and coupés based on the latest top-of-the-range medium saloon before long.

Of course, there was never any question of making the new Ponton-based coupés and cabriolets into best-sellers. Part of their appeal lay in the exclusivity which came from limited production, and in any case the market for cars at around 22,000DM was not large. Sales of the separate-chassis 220 cabriolets had averaged a few hundred each year, while just 85 coupés had been built in the single season of their production. As things were to turn out, the new overseas markets into which Mercedes moved during the 1950s helped to provide more sales for the Ponton coupés and cabriolets as well as for the everyday saloons, and around 1000 examples of the two-door Pontons were needed each year to satisfy demand.

Early schemes

The separate-chassis 220 two-doors could be had with three different bodies, a two/three-seater Cabriolet A, a five-seater Cabriolet C, and a two/three-seater coupé which was simply a Cabriolet A with a fixed roof. The same bodies – the coupé excepted – could also be bought on the 170S chassis, and Stuttgart seems to have started by examining the viability of replacing all three directly. Sketches drawn up in 1953 and based on 180 running gear show a five-seater Cabriolet B (with four side windows instead of the two on the Cabriolet C) on the standard wheelbase and a two/three-seater Cabriolet A on the short-wheelbase floorpan then being developed for the 190SL sports car. A coupé could no doubt have been developed easily from this.

But these early plans were rejected. The main reason was probably cost. Building both four-cylinder and six-cylinder two-door cars would entail the development of two new monocoques because the front-end structures of the two types would be different. If there were to be standard-wheelbase and short-wheelbase versions of each, the number of new monocoques would multiply to four. As monocoques were very much more expensive to develop than the bodies for separate-chassis cars, the whole exercise began to look prohibitively costly. Another factor in the decision may well have been that cabriolet derivatives of the four-cylinder cars were not expected to sell well; there had been no 170S two-door models since 1951, and they had not been much missed.

So Mercedes adopted a different strategy. First, there would be no four-cylinder two-doors, only six-cylinder types. Second, there would not be several new monocoques but just one, which would have to be very adaptable. And third, the cars would be given additional exclusivity by unique styling. The new monocoque was

Bearing the works code of W104, this full-size styling model for the Ponton cabriolet dates from November 1955. The side view shows it to have Mercedes' later styling trademark of vertical *Lichteinheiten* (combined lamp units) at the front, and also presents different chrome treatment from the production-like style on the other side of the model.

therefore designed so that it could be fitted out with front seats only to make a Cabriolet A; so that rear seats could be added to turn it into a Cabriolet C; and so that the addition of a steel roof would turn it into a coupé.

A new monocoque

Although the construction principles of the Ponton saloons were employed for the new monocoque, the two-doors actually had very little in common with their four-door counterparts. The Ponton floorpan was radically altered, with additional reinforcement to compensate for the absence of a roof, with its wheelbase shortened by 120mm (4.72in) to 2700mm (106.29in), and with a longer overhang behind the rear wheels. The styling was more adventurous than on the saloons, still slab-sided but altogether sleeker and less rounded, and although the radiator grille and headlamp treatment was unmistakably from the same family, the large rear lamps were much more stylised. In fact, they anticipated the restyled 300d limousines which would not be introduced until November 1957. Long doors were designed to allow ease

Another styling study, from early 1956, offers a Ponton cabriolet with peaked headlamps and a grille style reminiscent of the 190SL.

of entry into the rear seats, but they also contributed to the overall balance of the styling; to save weight, their steel skins were mounted on alloy frames.

The two-door Pontons had the latest style of wrap-round windscreen, and chrome trim running along the bottoms of the body sides and around the wheelarches was also very much in vogue – and dated quite quickly as the fashion for chrome excess waned in the early 1960s. Chrome trim strips were also used to outline the rear wing pressing and to decorate the otherwise relatively featureless body sides and front wing panels, where they had the valuable effect of decreasing the apparent height of the car. Later, when two-tone paintwork became optional, Ponton cabriolets finished in two colours had an additional curved chrome fillet just ahead of the front wheelarch to provide a boundary for the two colours.

In cabriolet form, the new monocoque looked very attractive from most angles, whether the top was up or stowed neatly behind the seats. Particular care had gone into the design of the soft-top itself, too, because this dispensed with the prominent external landau irons which had been a feature of earlier Mercedes cabriolets, and folded into a sunken well behind the seats so that it would not spoil the car's lines. Unfortunately, the steel coupé roof was altogether less successful. Anxious to give it the latest style of panoramic, wrap-round rear window, the Mercedes styling department seem to have overlooked the effect on the car's flowing lines of the very upright rear pillars which resulted. The result was a car which looked from some angles rather as if it had been fitted with a cheap after-market hard-top.

If the two-door Pontons appeared to offer rather less variety than their two-door predecessors, there was nevertheless plenty of scope for individualising cars through the Mercedes options list. The two/three-seater

Cabriolet A could be bought with individual seats, with reclining individual seats, or with a bench seat. In each case, the space behind the seats was fitted out as a luggage platform (although there was of course plenty of room in the boot as well). The Cabriolet C always had a two-passenger bench rear seat, but it could be had with the same three different varieties of front seat as the Cabriolet A. The coupés were strictly 2+2 models, but the rear bench seat folded down to create a luggage platform. They could also be equipped with a sliding steel sunroof.

Interiors in general were finished in the style which the buyers of such prestigious cars had come to expect. That meant leather upholstery, proper carpets rather than the rubber flooring found in Mercedes saloons, and wood and chrome on the dashboard. The front seats were thick and heavy armchairs, and their appearance contributed to the general air of luxury even if they were no softer to sit on than the seats in Mercedes saloons of the time.

On sale

The new cabriolet models were announced before the coupés, although in fact neither model was ready to go into production when a prototype 220 cabriolet was displayed on the Mercedes stand at the Frankfurt Motor Show in September 1955. Whether the company ever intended to offer the car in 220 form with the 85PS single-carburettor engine is debatable: the cabriolets were some 140kg (309lb) heavier than their saloon equivalents, which would not have given the sparkling performance which buyers of these expensive cars were entitled to expect. In practice, it was July 1956 before the first production cabriolets came off the assembly lines at Sindelfingen, and by then the twin-carburettor 220S had gone on sale.

Varieties of 220SE cabriolet colour treatments. Maroon 1958 car (note model name in centre of boot lid) with contrasting light-coloured top shows how elegance is retained when the top is raised; rare optional headrests are fitted. Two-tone paintwork became available on later cars, such as this extremely attractive 1959 model; only cabriolets had this two-tone pattern, divided along the chrome side strip with an extra chrome piece linking to the front wheel arch.

Ponton coupés and cabriolets were available with just two versions of the same 2195cc six-cylinder engine design: twin carburettors with 100/106PS for the 220S (left) or fuel injection with 115/120PS for the 220SE (right).

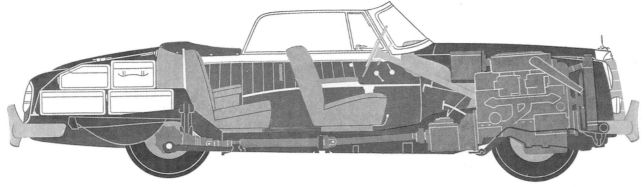

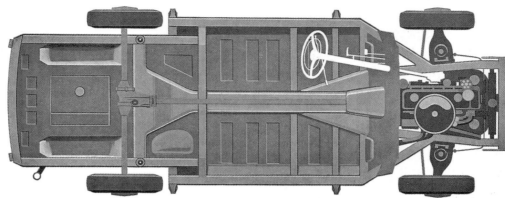

Packaging diagram from contemporary brochure shows that the 'Cabriolet C' could genuinely accommodate two adults in the back – although alternative 'Cabriolet A' specification had a luggage platform instead.

Rear seat contrasts. 'Cabriolet C' specification (left) provided this handsome place to sit; this is a prototype with an especially neat closing panel over the lowered top. The permanent roof made the coupé version more in the nature of a 2+2 (right); coupés always had a rear bench, but it could be folded to create a luggage platform.

So there never was a production 220 cabriolet, and the new body style went on sale with the twin-carburettor engine as a 220S. The slightly lighter coupé variant went on sale three months later, in October 1956.

Even with the twin-carburettor engine, the weight of the cabriolets and coupés counted against them. Their top speed was no greater than that of the 220S saloon, and their acceleration was also no better. Fuel consumption was marginally worse. Nevertheless, the wealthy businessmen, film stars and other lucky owners of these cars were clearly more concerned with style than

performance, because the two-door 220S cars certainly sold well enough.

As the two-doors were the top models of the medium-sized range, it was important that they should have the most powerful engine available. So when the injected 2.2-litre six-cylinder engine went into the new 220SE for the 1959 season, the twin-carburettor cabriolets and coupés went out of production and the 1959 cars also took on the injected engine and 220SE designation. That engine was uprated from 115PS to 120PS for the new 220SE Fintail saloon which was

Seen on a pre-1959 car with column gear shift and the early style of white steering wheel, the dashboard was lavishly finished with wood veneer. Details show the following: beautifully crafted wooden fillets on the doors; clock, radio and loudspeaker; the padded steering wheel (with black rim) and floor-mounted gear shift of post-1959 models; and chrome-framed door glass with the different pattern of two-tone colour split found on coupés.

announced in the autumn of 1959, and the 120bhp engine was fitted to the two-door Pontons at the same time, thus ensuring that the most prestigious models still had the best possible performance.

The 220SE coupés and cabriolets remained in production for just one year after the six-cylinder Ponton saloons had been replaced by six-cylinder Fintail models, and the last examples were built in November 1960.

There was then a gap of a few months before the announcement of the new two-door models which paralleled the Fintails.

In four seasons of full production, a total of 5371 Ponton coupé and cabriolet models were built, the cabriolets outnumbering the coupés by about three to two. Only small numbers were built with right-hand drive, and the cars were always rare even in Germany.

FINTAIL SALOONS

M ercedes never gave the name 'Fintails' to the cars they developed to replace the Ponton saloons of the 1950s. To the design engineers and production workers alike, they were W110, W111 and W112 models. However, these were cars designed in a period when the world looked up to American car styling and when Mercedes in particular was trying hard to break into the American market. So they embodied elements of contemporary US styling, and among these elements were discreet tail fins. The nickname of 'Fintails' was therefore inevitable, and had the advantage of being much easier to use than the official factory designations!

These cars were also built during a period of great expansion for Mercedes-Benz. They were made in huge numbers – nearly 973,000 were built in eight seasons of production – and sold all over the world as Mercedes moved into new territories. So familiar did they become in the 1960s that it was (and still is) easy to forget that they embodied a number of very important engineering advances. These were the cars which other manufacturers around the world looked up to and attempted to emulate, and they had a powerful impact on the industry.

Top of the range Fintail saloon from 1961 was the technically advanced W112 300SE, with air suspension and fuel-injected all-alloy 3-litre engine. Although German-registered, this example has the twin headlamps normally found only on US-market cars. The badge was distinguishable even at a distance by its unique 'frame'.

What, then, were the engineering advances which the Fintails brought with them? Probably the most important of all was the concept of the crash-resistant bodyshell combined with a wealth of safety features. All the Fintail models also featured the overhead camshaft engine layout which Mercedes had pioneered as long ago as 1951 (the last side-valve Mercedes engine was built in 1957 and the last pushrod overhead-valve type in 1961). They continued to demonstrate the viability of diesel engines for passenger cars when few other manufacturers showed any interest whatsoever, they demonstrated Mercedes'

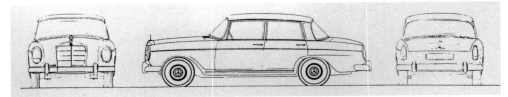

Apparently dated 1956, this is an early design drawing for the Fintail saloon. It still bears strong traces of the Ponton design.

For decades Mercedes has put a great deal of research and development effort into its cars. Proper crash tests started in 1959, and from 1962 a steam rocket was used to propel cars into a solid wall to test collision performance. The other scene shows a Fintail six-cylinder linked to a mobile laboratory (based on a 300 saloon) by an 'umbilical cord'.

continuing commitment to fuel injection systems, and they experimented with all-alloy engines. They continued to use all-round coil-spring independent suspension while many manufacturers were still committed to leaf-sprung beam rear axles, they brought to Mercedes a new generation of swing-axle suspension with a horizontal compensating spring, and they bravely experimented with air suspension. They introduced the 'clap-hands' windscreen wiper system, which cleaned a greater proportion of the screen than conventional parallel wipers, and last, but not least (in two areas where Mercedes lagged behind other makers), they introduced automatic transmission and disc brakes to the medium-sized Mercedes.

Design

The project to design a 'new 220', as Chief Engineer Fritz Nallinger called it, was not started until 1956. Much of the engineering dated from earlier than that, however, because many of the Fintails' chassis and drivetrain components were carried over from the Ponton models, albeit in further developed form. In addition, the ideas behind the Fintails' crash-resistant bodyshells dated back to 1951 – and had already been seen in the Ponton models – when Mercedes had patented engineer Béla Barényi's concept of a rigid central passenger cell with impact-absorbing 'crumple zones' in front and behind.

It is notable that the six-cylinder car was seen as the

most important one in the range right from the beginning. Mercedes had learned from the experience of the Pontons that prestige-conscious six-cylinder buyers were not amused to discover they were still being offered an old design (the 220) when buyers of the cheaper four-cylinder cars (the 180) were offered the latest one. So this time, the product strategy was different. The six-cylinder cars would be introduced first and would run alongside the older Ponton four-cylinders. Four-cylinder models of the new design would then follow – and, as things were to turn out, there would be a third stage when the range would move into a new market area with an additional model positioned above the 2.2-litre six-cylinder cars.

The structure of the new cars followed the principles established with the Ponton saloons in its unitary construction with the engine and front suspension mounted on a detachable subframe. The bodyshell incorporated the same rigid central passenger cell with front and rear crumple zones, but the subframe was rather simpler in design than the Ponton type. Front suspension was essentially the same as before, with unequal-length wishbones and coil springs, although the track was wider, the dampers were located further outboard, and an anti-roll bar permitted rather softer springing for an American-style 'boulevard' ride. This was matched by softer springs at the rear, where one swing-axle was sprung against the other to prevent excessive roll by a horizontally-mounted coil spring above the

Wollen Sie große Worte
oder größere Sicherheit?

THE **MERCEDES-BENZ 220SE**
CAN DO THINGS OTHER CARS CANNOT

This picture demonstrates a very unusual feature of the Mercedes-Benz 220SE. (E means Einspritzmotor...fuel injection.) Unlike most cars, Mercedes-Benz has four-wheel independent suspension for safer cornering and greater comfort. Moreover, its rear axle (a swing axle) employs a horizontal spring, perfected in racing for cornering. The 220SE can keep its equilibrium when other cars start to slide.

There's something else the 220SE can do for you and your passengers. It adds, to the creature comforts and spirited performance of the car, the indefinable pride of motoring behind the silver star of Mercedes-Benz.

MERCEDES-BENZ SALES, INC.
SEE MERCEDES-BENZ CARS AT YOUR NEAREST DEALER

WE CAN ALSO ARRANGE FOR 1961 EUROPEAN DELIVERY. WE WILL SERVICE YOUR CAR ON YOUR RETURN HOME.

MOTOR TREND/JUNE 1961 17

Contrasting messages in two Fintail adverts. While the German emphasis was on safety, the Americans were being sold performance as well. The 220S and 220SE were available with optional two-tone paintwork (below), which added a little more glamour.

differential. It was not a complete success, however, because the softer rear springs were not up to the weight of a full boot and so the cars tended to drag their tails when laden. Later in production, Mercedes had to introduce methods of compensating for those soft rear springs.

The basic shape of the new 220, or W111 saloon, was settled during 1957 by Karl Wilfert's stylists. It appears that they had started with a set of passenger compartment dimensions provided by Fritz Nallinger, and the car they drew up around these dimensions had very different proportions indeed from the Ponton saloons. Despite its longer passenger compartment, it had a shorter wheelbase of 2750mm (108.3in) as compared to the Ponton 220's 2820mm (111in) wheelbase, and yet it was also longer than the 4715mm (187in) Ponton at 4875mm (191.9in) thanks to a much larger boot. It was also lower and wider than the car it was to replace – and in those dimensions it is not hard to see Mercedes following the dictates of the contemporary American 'longer, lower, wider' styling progression!

Decoration was also resolutely American in inspiration, although the car's overall shape suggested the straight lines favoured by Italian stylists of the time. The tail fins were most definitely inspired by American designs, although Mercedes had hedged their bets by not making them too large, and the heavy chrome bumpers with additional quarter bumpers above them at the front again suggested the American school of styling. The large stylised rear lamp units also made clear that Stuttgart's stylists had been looking carefully at what was happening on the other side of the Atlantic.

Yet the car retained identifiable Mercedes styling features. The distinctive grille was the most obvious, while

alongside it stood the vertical *Lichteinheiten* (or combined lamp units) first seen on the 1957 300SL roadster. These combined headlamp, fog lamp and direction indicator lamp under a single glass cover, and would go on to become a Mercedes styling trademark of the 1960s. Sadly, they did not meet new American lighting regulations, though, and so Fintails destined for the USA had a distinctive arrangement of two round sealed-beam headlamps stacked one above the other, with the turn indicator lamp relocated between headlamps and grille. This suited the Americans, who thought that it was a European interpretation of the twin-headlamp style pioneered on the 1957 Lincolns!

The first hand-built W111 took to the roads in January 1958, and this car and its many sisters covered some two million test miles before pilot production of the new Fintail models began during May 1959 in preparation for the public announcement at the Frankfurt Motor Show in September.

When they went out on public roads, the test cars were rather clumsily disguised with dummy round grilles, very basic rear lights and olive drab paint in order not to attract the attention of 'spy' photographers working for the motoring press. However, several of them *were* recognised for what they were, and photographs appeared in a number of magazines.

The core model of the Fintail range introduced in 1959 was the W111 220S, which had a more powerful version of the M180 six-cylinder engine also fitted to the 220. As the badge on the boot lid makes clear, this example has Mercedes' own four-speed automatic transmission. This restored car also has incorrect 14in (not 13in) wheels with 'flat-face' hub caps, from a later W108.

New for 1960: 220, 220S and 220SE

Mercedes employed the same names for the six-cylinder Fintail saloons introduced at the 1959 Frankfurt Show as they had for the Ponton models which the new cars replaced. So the pecking order started with the 220 (which really replaced the old 219) and went on up through the 220S to the top-model 220SE with fuel injection. Within the Mercedes organisation, the cars

actually carried a b-suffix to distinguish them from the a-suffix Ponton six-cylinders, but of course this was not reflected in their badges.

All three models had the seven-bearing, overhead camshaft six-cylinder engine with the same 2195cc swept volume, and in all cases the engine was more powerful than in the Ponton models of the same name. Even the entry-level 220 now had twin carburettors to give 95PS, while the 220S had two twin-choke carburettors and

When the W110 four-cylinder cars were introduced in 1961, they came with a short-nose – and today more dated-looking – edition of the Fintail body. Round headlamps and single bumpers were differences.

110PS at a slightly higher engine speed. The 220SE, meanwhile, once again had Bosch fuel injection, now tuned to deliver 120PS instead of the older car's 115PS. With lower axle ratios than the 220, the 220S and 220SE accelerated noticeably better, but their more powerful engines also gave them higher top speeds. Fuel consumption was much the same for all three models, at a rather thirsty 14 litres for every 100km (16.8mpg).

There were other equipment differences, of course. Brakes were finned drums all round on all three models, but only the 220S and 220SE had a servo as standard; that was an extra-cost option on the 220. Power steering was available, too, but cost extra on all models. Buyers also wanted it to be obvious when they had paid the extra for one of the more up-market models, and so Mercedes had used the familiar trick of loading the more expensive models with more chrome. The 220 had small hubcaps and a single rear bumper, but the 220S and 220SE both had full-size wheel trims and double rear bumpers with separate number plate lights. They also had extra chrome around their rear lamps, chrome on the scuttle air intake, and chrome strips along the top of their rear fins. To distinguish 220SE from 220S, however, onlookers had to peer at the badge on the boot lid: just as on the six-

cylinder Pontons, Mercedes had chosen not to make a clear visual distinction between the top-model fuel-injected car and its mid-range sister.

These were particularly spacious cars, and the large glass area with deep side windows and wrap-round front and rear screens made their passenger compartments feel even larger than they actually were. The seats were large and comfortable, if a little hard on first acquaintance, and were upholstered as usual in MB-Tex vinyl or in woolcloth; leather was an extra-cost option and came with perforated panels which allowed the seats to 'breathe'. The front seats were Reutter recliners on the 220S and 220SE, but had fixed backrests unless to special order on the 220. Mercedes' concern for passive safety was evident throughout, too, as all hard edges had been eliminated, the minor switches were crushable, the interior mirror had a breakaway stem, and there was padding on the dash top and steering wheel centre.

Buyers could ask for the gear lever to be located either on the floor or on the steering column, and the Hydrak clutch was optional on all three models. Sadly, the handbrake still lived under the dash to suit American tastes, and the new instrument panel was neither an aesthetic nor an ergonomic success. It was dominated by a vertical strip-type speedometer, which proved hard to read and was roundly criticised by the motoring press. Few people liked the fake wood on the dashboard, either, although Mercedes insisted that it was safer than real wood because it would not splinter in a collision!

The 190, 190D and 300SE

It would be some 18 months before Mercedes introduced any further Fintail models. The six-cylinder models introduced for the 1960 model year had been extremely well-received, and the painstaking development which had gone into them reaped its own reward when there proved no need to make hasty modifications. Instead, Stuttgart's engineers spent most of 1960 refining the four-cylinder Fintail range and developing a new and even more expensive six-cylinder model which would take its place above the 220SE in April 1961.

The four-cylinder models were expected, of course. The Ponton four-cylinders had held the fort since 1959, but in June 1961 production began of the cars which would replace them. There would be no replacements, however, for the cheapest 180 and 180D: the new cars moved the entry level of the Mercedes range up a notch and were badged as 190 and 190D. In the Mercedes scheme of things, they were W110 models, and they had a new short-nose edition of the Fintail bodyshell.

Perhaps deliberately, in order not to deter the legions of taxi drivers who had come to depend on a diesel Mercedes, the front end of the new short-nose shell looked very much like the front end of a four-cylinder Ponton. It had the same large Mercedes grille, and ordinary round headlamps instead of the six-cylinders' stylish *Lichteinheiten*. Indicators and parking lamps sprouted from the wing tops just ahead of the windscreen, just as they had on the four-cylinder Pontons, and in many ways the short-nose car looked rather like a hybrid, with little of the grace of the six-cylinder design.

None of that deterred the buyers. Taxi drivers loved the additional interior space of the new design and its larger boot, and they also appreciated the extra power and torque of the 190D's new 2-litre (1988cc) diesel engine. The engine's basic design was unchanged, but an extra 2mm of bore diameter provided the capacity increase. It mattered: the Fintail 190D was a heavier car than the Ponton model it replaced and needed the bigger engine as well as deeper gearing to maintain the older car's acceleration. And even though its maximum speed was slightly higher, the Fintail 190D was also noticeably thirstier than the car it replaced.

The new petrol 190, however, showed improvements all round. It certainly was heavier than the Ponton 190, but with a mildly altered version of the same 1.9-litre (1897cc) engine and slightly taller overall gearing, it accelerated faster, reached a higher top speed, and

returned the same overall fuel consumption. That was a considerable achievement, and just as other manufacturers pored over the new six-cylinder cars to learn from the Stuttgart design, so they dissected the 190 to discover its secrets. None managed to emulate them in the short term, though, and the 190 remained exemplary throughout its production life even though it was outsold massively by its diesel sister.

The new six-cylinder car was actually introduced two months before the four-cylinder models, and represented some new thinking from Mercedes. The company had by this stage recognised that the market for limousines like its 300 was shrinking, and had conceived a two-pronged strategy to replace them. First, it planned to offer a 3-litre Fintail derivative with a very high specification to cater for those who mostly drove themselves; and second, it had started work on the big 600, a formal and massively expensive chauffeur-driven limousine which would become the company's flagship. Both cars would incorporate a wealth of new technology, and the plan was to introduce the higher-volume Fintail model first.

The car's name of 300SE chose itself, as it had an injected 3-litre engine. This was based on the overhead camshaft unit which had powered the 300 since 1951 and was also used in the 300SL sports models, but there was one very important difference. The iron-block, alloy-head 3-litre engine was a big and heavy piece of machinery, and the Mercedes engineers probably believed it was too heavy to put into the Fintail saloon shell without upsetting the balance of the car. So the engine designers working under Josef Müller redeveloped the engine with an alloy cylinder block incorporating press-fit dry liners. This saved no less than 40kg (88lb). However, Mercedes did not solve the problem of noise properly before putting the all-alloy engine into production, and the 300SE could sound quite harsh at speed as a result. All-alloy American engines of the time, such as the Buick 215 V8 (later adopted by Rover in Britain), did not suffer from this problem because their rev limits were generally lower.

The iron-block 3-litre engine was already being built with Bosch fuel injection for the 300 limousine and the 300SL, but Mercedes chose not to offer the alloy-block derivative with the individual port injection used in the 300SL to give maximum power. Instead, there was a less efficient – and less costly – manifold injection system, similar to the one used in the 220SE. In this form, it delivered the same 160PS as the injected iron-block engine in the 300d limousine, at a slightly lower crankshaft speed. As the big limousine was considerably heavier than the Fintail saloon, performance proved more

Everybody's favourite image of a four-cylinder Fintail: the ubiquitous taxi. This one is not quite what it seems, for it is a factory-built prototype of an 'attack-proof' taxi, with a fixed armoured-glass partition to protect the driver from rowdy rear-seat passengers. They paid their fare through a sliding tray in the division. The driving compartment, however, could easily belong to any other 190D-based taxi.

than adequate, with a 180km/h (112mph) top speed even with the standard automatic transmission.

This automatic transmission was a first for Mercedes. The only one of the company's products available with automatic before the 300SE was the 300 limousine, optionally available with a three-speed automatic after 1955. However, that was so rare as to be almost non-existent, and most Mercedes customers of the time would probably have believed that the company had never offered an automatic. As it was, Stuttgart's engineers were not very happy with the performance of the three-speed automatic, arguing that the torque converter was wasteful of power. So they set about developing a new automatic transmission, this time with the same four speeds as a conventional manual gearbox, and this time using a fluid coupling to cushion the changes instead of a torque converter – a solution they believed to be less wasteful of engine power.

The Mercedes four-speed automatic worked well enough with the ample torque of the 3-litre engine, but

was less successful when in later years it was used with smaller engines. It did not suit all the 300SE's customers, either, and a number asked for their cars to be supplied with manual gearboxes. Mercedes complied – the 300SE was more or less built to order anyway – and within two years found itself obliged to offer manual as a catalogued alternative, together with a choice of axle ratios.

There was much more of engineering interest in the 300SE than its drivetrain. To stop this high-performance Fintail effectively, Mercedes fitted it with Dunlop disc brakes on all four wheels, together with a vacuum servo as standard. To prevent wheelspin, they standardised a limited-slip differential (although supply difficulties meant that the first 11 months' production was supplied without it), and it almost went without saying that power-assisted steering was also standard. This latter, though, was available on cheaper Mercedes models; the 300SE's air suspension was not.

During the development of the Fintails, Mercedes had paid special attention to making the cars' ride soft enough to appeal to American tastes, yet without detriment to the very much tauter handling which European customers expected. For the 300SE, they decided to go one better by fitting the car with an all-new air suspension system. The US market must have been firmly in view: Cadillac had offered air suspension as an option on its 1958 models, but the system had been so prone to malfunctions that its benefits to ride comfort were swiftly forgotten.

No other manufacturer attempted to make air suspension work, but Bosch in Germany kept plugging away at an air suspension system and in 1959 this appeared on the top-of-the-range six-cylinder Borgward. Mercedes-Benz probably saw red at this, as it represented technical one-upmanship for a rival manufacturer. They,

As the top-of-the-range model, the 300SE used the most powerful engine installed in the Fintails – a fuel-injected all-alloy 3-litre six-cylinder developing 160PS before 1964 and 170PS thereafter.

too, chose to work with Bosch, and it was a more advanced version of the Bosch system which appeared on the 300SE in 1961. Ironically, that was the year when Borgward went out of business, after selling only small numbers of their cars with the air suspension option.

The Bosch air suspension consisted of four rubber bags, which were fitted in place of conventional steel springs and were kept inflated by an engine-driven compressor. Axle sensors and complex interlinking ensured that the air suspension kept the 300SE's body level at all times, although it could not react fast enough to cornering roll and so anti-roll bars were fitted both front and rear. The air suspension provided a quite remarkably soft and well-controlled ride, but although it was fairly durable it did need regular maintenance. This proved too much for some owners, and after using the

Details of the sumptuous 300SE: dashboard with heavy padding top and bottom; vertical strip-type speedometer (used on all Fintail saloons) is clear and practical, but was not universally liked; soft fabric and acres of space in the rear seat; subtle use of wood trim on the doors was confined to 3-litre models; details of abundant chrome trimming, seen on a fin (as used on all six-cylinder saloons) and D pillar air vents (normal-wheelbase 300SE only).

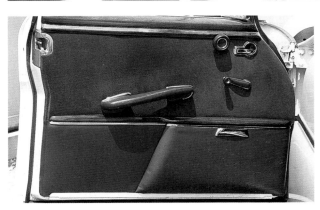

To distinguish the long-wheelbase 300SE – launched in 1963 – from its standard-wheelbase sister, Mercedes actually removed some of the chrome: look at the rear window pillar. Otherwise, the only way of telling that this was the limousine version of the car was to take a careful look at the rear door window, which was longer than on the standard 300SE. The styling is so well-balanced that the extra 100mm is almost undetectable at first sight.

system again on the W109 300SEL between 1965-67, Mercedes abandoned it.

All these new engineering features on the 300SE were matched by luxury touches. Leather seats and a wood-faced dashboard were standard, and air conditioning was optional. A courtesy light delay and a telescopic radio aerial which extended electrically when the radio was switched on were not common features on other cars until more than 20 years later, but they were both standard on the 300SE. And Mercedes did not disappoint those 300SE customers who wanted onlookers to know that they had bought the expensive top-of-the-range car and not one of the cheaper variants. The 300SE could be instantly distinguished from the other Fintail saloons by bright trim running round the wheelarches and along the body sills, by extra chrome on the air outlet vents behind the side windows, and by chromed twin tail-pipes.

1962: disc brakes, automatic transmissions and utility bodies

Mercedes recognised that disc brakes would inevitably replace drum brakes as cars became capable of higher speeds, and so in April 1962 they standardised front discs on the servo-equipped 220S and 220SE models, although these cars retained drum brakes at the rear. Similarly convinced of the merits and the sales potential of its new automatic transmission, the company extended its availability to the other six-cylinder Fintails and to the petrol-engined 190 in August 1962 for the 1963 season,

and withdrew the unpopular Hydrak automatic clutch option. A few months later, in the spring of 1963, the automatic transmission was even made optional on the 190D model, where its effect on performance was less marked than might have been expected. It did cause a noticeable increase in fuel consumption, however, just as it did on the petrol-engined models.

It was also during 1962 that the company began to supply rolling chassis to the coachbuilders who had constructed ambulances and Kombi estate cars on the Ponton models. The brief from Mercedes to the Binz and Miesen companies was presumably to produce Fintail editions of the models they had made so successfully before, because both companies came up with four-door estate-type bodies which could be equipped as ambulances or sold as Kombi estates. As the ambulances and estates were likely to be called upon to carry heavier loads than the saloons, Mercedes equipped their rolling chassis with larger 15in wheels.

Although the two coachbuilders each designed the same type of body, their interpretations of the requirement were quite distinctively different from each other. The Miesen body, for example, had a high loading sill at the rear, a flattish roof and retained the standard saloon tail lamps. The Binz body, by contrast, had a curved roof, a tailgate which reached down to bumper level, and a utilitarian cluster of small circular tail lamps. These two types remained available on the 190 and 190D rolling chassis through to the end of production in 1965, when 200 and 200D editions took over. Production ended with the last Fintails in 1968, and precise totals are not available. The majority of these vehicles were fitted out as ambulances, particularly after 1966 when the new Universal estate by IMA joined the Fintail range.

The long-wheelbase 300SE

Mercedes never felt obliged to introduce new models at the Frankfurt Motor Show on their home territory if there was a better opportunity at another time of the year. Unwilling to detract from the impact of the planned 230SL sports car at the 1963 Show, the company therefore decided to announce that year's other major new model six months earlier at the Geneva Motor Show. This was a long-wheelbase edition of the 300SE.

It was the loss of the old 300 limousine which had

Befitting a car that was often chauffeur-driven, the long-wheelbase 300SE could be ordered with an electrically operated central dividing partition, which in the UK added £159 10s to the car's £4400 price tag.

prompted the development of this new model. The old car had stopped production in March 1962 and, although the Fintail 300SE was ready and waiting to field the 300's owner-driver customers, there was now nothing in the Mercedes range to cater for the chauffeur-driven market. The new 600 limousine would not go into production until autumn 1964 (although Mercedes whetted appetites by showing a prototype at the Paris Motor Show a year before that), and so the long-wheelbase 300SE was developed to bridge the gap. In fact, it carved out its own market, and a long-wheelbase version of the top-model Mercedes saloon became a permanent feature of the range for the next 30 years.

The long-wheelbase 300SE was simply a standard 300SE with 100mm (3.94in) inserted into the wheelbase in the rear footwell area. The additional space gave the rear passengers the sort of lounging room expected in a chauffeur-driven car, but the additional metal also added weight, and the extra 50kg damaged the fuel consumption and took some of the sparkle from its off-the-line acceleration. Aiming to counter those problems, Mercedes fitted the long-wheelbase car with a lower first gear and a larger 82-litre fuel tank which at least lengthened the touring range. This new tank was also fitted to the standard-wheelbase 300SE.

The usual Mercedes ploy to distinguish the top-of-the-range model from cheaper variants was to load it with extra chrome. However, the standard-wheelbase 300SE was already so heavily chromed that to have added more for the long-wheelbase car would have been

ridiculous. So Mercedes took the opposite course of action, and deleted the chrome around the air vents on the long-wheelbase model while adding a little more around the side windows. Even so, it was not easy to recognise a long-wheelbase 300SE at a distance, and even the longer rear doors were not immediately obvious.

Better brakes for 1964 and the end of an era in 1965

The disc front brakes introduced on the 220S and 220SE in April 1962 had proved wholly successful, and so Mercedes standardised them across the range for the 1964 season which began with the Frankfurt Show in September 1963. The higher pedal pressures which they needed meant that servos had to be fitted to those models which had not previously had them, and at the same time Mercedes upgraded the braking systems on all Fintail models by fitting dual-circuit hydraulics. This was a safety measure well in advance of its adoption elsewhere, and ensured that there would always be some braking available even if there was a loss of fluid somewhere in the system.

For 1964, there was also a minor improvement to the 220S, which gained new Zenith carburettors and an automatic choke. In addition, supplementary air springs on the rear axle were made available at extra cost for all Fintail models, in order to prevent a laden boot from overcoming the soft coil springs and causing the rear end to sag. Then, in January 1964, the engines of both 300SE models were given higher compression ratios and a more efficient port-injection system with a new six-plunger fuel pump. These modifications raised maximum power by 10PS to give higher maximum speeds, and although maximum torque was slightly reduced, off-the-line acceleration was also improved. A taller 3.75:1 axle ratio was also introduced as an option, so that it was possible in the standard-wheelbase car to reach a genuine maximum of 200km/h (124mph) – an astonishing speed for a luxury saloon in the mid-1960s.

In May 1964, power-assisted steering was standardised on the two four-cylinder models, but plans were already well advanced for the introduction of the second-generation Fintail models in 1965, and so no more changes of any significance were made. Production of the best-selling 220S and of the standard-wheelbase 300SE was first to stop, in July 1965, and the last 190, 190D, 220, 220SE and long-wheelbase 300SE cars were built in August. With effect from the Frankfurt Show which opened the following month, the whole of the Fintail saloon range would be renewed.

It was not easy to distinguish a second-generation model from a first-generation type, but there were differences post-1965. At the front (period publicity shot of a 230, a new 'hybrid' model using the six-cylinder engine in the short-nosed four-cylinder body) were rather inelegant combined indicator/sidelamp clusters below the headlamps. At the rear (recent shot of a 200) there were updated lights and extra chrome on the rear pillar air vents and below the boot lid, although four-cylinder models still had much less ornate trim around the tail than their six-cylinder sisters.

Second generation: 200s and 230s

Ever since the early 1950s, it has been Mercedes policy to plan for long production runs. New models are generally fitted in the beginning with engines which are already half-way through their production life, and then are re-engined half-way through their own production lives.

That way, Mercedes never has to take the risk of introducing completely new engines and completely new cars at the same time. So, rather more than mid-way through their production lives, the Fintails were re-engined in 1965. However, other factors also influenced the changes which took place that year.

Mercedes had clearly been struggling to distinguish

In its brochures for the second-generation four-cylinder models, Mercedes emphasised the practical aspects of ownership, showing a 200 during hot climate testing in Africa and a 200D on a 4073-mile 'Trans-Europe Economy Test'. Unfortunately the consumption achieved by the diesel engine during this exercise was not disclosed, although the normal average figure quoted was 35.3mpg.

Dashboards remained largely unchanged from the first-generation cars, but redesigned door trims for the 200, 200D and 230 brought useful storage pockets. Among the new power units introduced in 1965 was this five-bearing four-cylinder M121 for the petrol-engined 200; all engines now had alternators.

the most expensive derivatives of the Fintail range from the mid-range models. A few pieces of chrome were the only external differences between the best-selling 220S and the much more expensive and exclusive 300SE, and even the long-wheelbase 300SE was not very distinctive. Customers for the more expensive models objected to this, and Mercedes knew that it was costing them sales. So the company's stylists were asked to examine ways of making the top models look different from the mid-range saloons. None of the solutions found favour, and in the end Stuttgart decided to split the range into two and to develop a completely new bodyshell for the more expensive models. This, coded W108 (or W109 for the long-wheelbase variant with air suspension), was introduced at the Frankfurt Show in September 1965. Mercedes had decided to make the cut-off point between the Fintails and the new range at 2.5 litres, and the new cars consisted of 250S, 250SE, 300SE and 300SEL (long-wheelbase) models.

So there was no need to replace the two 300SE Fintail models, and the 220SE was replaced by the new 250SE. The four models up to and including the 220S, however, were directly replaced: the 190 and 190D by a 200 and 200D, the 220 by a 230, and the 220S by a 230S. Just as they had created a hybrid mid-range model with the Ponton 219, so Mercedes did the same with the Fintail 230, equipping the short-nose bodyshell with a six-cylinder engine.

All the engines were new to the Fintail range, and all of them had alternators instead of dynamos – a first for Mercedes. Even the engine in the 200D had been improved, for although it had the same 1988cc swept volume as the superseded 190D engine and the same 55PS maximum power, it had been redeveloped to give

smoother running with five main bearings instead of the earlier three. As for the petrol engine in the 200, that had been bored out from the 1897cc of the 190 to the same 1988cc as the diesel engine had. It delivered a lot more power – 95PS as against 80PS – and it also had five main bearings instead of the earlier engine's three. Acceleration and maximum speed were very much better, but the downside was increased fuel consumption.

The two six-cylinder cars both had variants of the same engine. This was a big-bore development of the old 2.2-litre engine, and it had first been seen in the 1963 230SL sports car, when it was fitted with Bosch injection. In the 230, it had two Solex carburettors and 105PS; in the 230S, it came with two Zenith carburettors, a different camshaft and 120PS. The new engine endowed both Fintail saloons with slightly better performance than their predecessors had enjoyed – and, of course, standardisation of the 2.3-litre block for the 230SL, 230 and 230S allowed Mercedes to make production economies as it no longer had to manufacture the old 2.2-litre block as well.

The 200, 200D and 230 were easy enough to tell from the earlier short-nose Fintail saloons, because they had large new light clusters underneath their headlamps. These clusters combined small fog lamps with large turn indicators, and were perhaps an improvement over the

older combined parking and indicator lamps perched on top of the wings, although they would certainly not have won any prizes for appearance. These second-generation short-nose W110s also had extra chrome on their boot lids and around the air outlet vents behind the side windows, and inside they had rather plusher seats than before.

Equipment levels on the 230S, though, had been downgraded as compared to the 220S it replaced, in order to protect sales of the 250S which was the entry-level model of the new and more expensive S-class range. The 230S had simpler interior trim than the 220S, and a toughened glass windscreen instead of a laminated type. It came with manual steering rather than the power-assisted type standard on the 220S, and that steering was rather lower-geared than on the earlier cars to offset the effects of the new model's 60kg weight increase.

Power steering was optional on all the second-generation cars, and all of them had new fuel tanks with a 65-litre capacity instead of the previous models' 51 litres. The supplementary air suspension option for the rear axle was no longer available, and was replaced by a cheaper and less complicated Boge self-levelling strut, which pumped up when the car was heavily laden in order to maintain the correct suspension height. This strut was made standard on the 230S, but was an extra-cost option on the other three Fintail saloons.

1966: an upgraded 230 and a new Kombi

Sales of the 230 took off in a big way, and the car quickly became more popular than the 220 it had replaced. Sales soared even higher when the more powerful 230S engine was fitted in autumn 1966 for the 1967 season. The 230S, however, never emulated sales of the 220S. Buyers were probably tempted by the new and more sophisticated 250S, which was attractively priced in Germany, where it cost 15,300DM as against the 14,000DM of the 230S.

The main news for the 1967 season, however, was the introduction in late 1966 of new Universal estate models, available as derivatives of all four Fintail saloons. These were actually converted by the Belgian coachworks IMA S.A. in Brussels, and were built like the Binz and Miesen

The Universal estate was a conversion built by IMA in Brussels, this example a six-cylinder 230S; note the 15in wheels and special tail-lamp clusters, which integrated very neatly with the existing styling. The W110 ambulance is typical of the conversions carried out by Binz, mainly on the standard-wheelbase platform, but it has a most curious combination of pre-1965 and post-1965 indicators – on top of the wings *and* below the headlamps!

ambulance conversions on rolling chassis supplied by Stuttgart. The Universal estates had 15in wheels, just like the ambulances, and they had heavy-duty rear suspension with the Boge self-levelling strut as standard.

The Universal estate models came with a full Mercedes-Benz warranty and were sold to special order through the company's dealers. Options included a split-folding rear seat – rare and quite advanced thinking for the middle 1960s – and a rearward-facing occasional bench seat in the load bed which folded away when not in use. These estates were quite pleasing to look at, as their new rear quarters blended well with the lines of the standard Fintail saloon body. They were also easy to distinguish from the earlier Miesen and Binz estates because they had unique stylised triangular rear lamp clusters. Production figures are not available, but the cars were certainly made in only small numbers.

The seven/eight-seater airport taxi was introduced by the coachbuilders Binz in May 1967. The centre row of seats folded forwards to provide access to the rear.

Final fling: the seven-seater 200D

Perhaps worried that the new IMA Universal estate might be developed into an ambulance and so take over their market, the coachbuilders Binz came up with an adventurous new variant on the Fintail saloon in May 1967. This was a seven-seater airport taxi, with its wheelbase extended by no less than 650mm (25.59in) so that a third row of seats could be fitted in the middle. As it was aimed at the taxi market, the seven-seater was made available only in diesel form and was always badged as a 200D. Unfortunately, the extra 140kg (309lb) weight that it carried were more than the 2-litre diesel engine could comfortably handle. Although the seven-seater 200D had a claimed top speed of 125km/h (78mph), such a speed was only realistically obtainable on a long motorway run, and acceleration could best be described as leisurely, especially when the taxi was carrying its full complement of passengers.

Like the ambulances and Kombi estates, the seven-seater was built on rolling chassis shipped out from Stuttgart and equipped with 15in wheels. A self-levelling strut on the rear axle was standard but power steering – perhaps surprisingly – was not. It is not clear how many of these unwieldy monsters were built, but there cannot have been many. Production of the 200D ended at Stuttgart in February 1968, just nine months after the seven-seater had been announced. In the same month, the 200 and 230 also ceased production, while the top-model 230S had gone in January. That month, Mercedes had announced its new mid-range saloons, the W114 six-cylinder and W115 four-cylinder models. Those would go on to enjoy even greater sales success than the Fintails had known, although it is certainly debatable whether they ever had quite as much character as the W110, W111 and W112 saloons built between 1959 and 1968.

A handsome 300SE doing what it was designed for: transporting captains of industry in chauffeur-driven splendour.

W111 AND W112
COUPÉS AND CABRIOLETS

The Mercedes design and production cycle in the mid-1950s was such that there was barely time to note the sales response to a new range of models before beginning work on its eventual successor. So it was with the cars which were to replace the Ponton coupés and cabriolets of the later 1950s, because these cars entered production in 1956 and work started on their successors the following year.

However, there was a wind of change blowing through the corridors in Stuttgart. Daimler-Benz management had already recognised that its range of models had become rather too complicated, and was looking at what are now called economies of scale by reducing the number of individual types in production while retaining and, ideally, expanding the client-base. One particular problem was that there were too many

The 220SE coupé (above) appeared seven months before the cabriolet (right) equivalent in 1961. The coupé is an American model, with the twin round headlamps unique to that market.

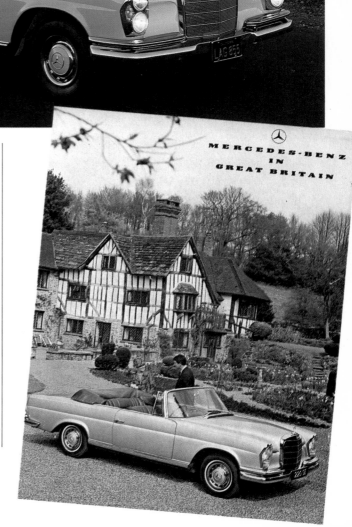

Design stages. Paul Bracq sketch of 1957 shows American influence in exaggerated wrap-round of front and rear screens – and production-like fins. The 1959 prototype looks close to the real thing, but a few detail touches – rear pillar vents, tail lights – remain to be resolved.

low-volume models in production; the Ponton coupés and cabriolets were among these, but the separate-chassis 300S coupé and roadster models were made in even smaller numbers. These hugely expensive machines were built by hand and were affordable usually only by crowned heads of state, which inevitably limited the numbers which could be sold. They were also going to become due for replacement before long, having been in production since 1952.

So a new and ambitious plan was drawn up. Instead of replacing the two-door Pontons and the 300S models by two new ranges, Mercedes would design a single new range to replace both of them. It was a gamble – not least because those used to the exclusivity of a 300S might not take kindly to seeing its replacement as part of a range which included cheaper lookalike models – but sales figures show that the plan succeeded only too well. The Ponton-derived two-doors sold an average of 1074 cars a year during their production life, while the 300S models averaged only 95 cars a year; together, these made for a yearly average of 1169 cars. The new 'combined' range which replaced them sold an average of 3748 cars a year during the first seven years in production – well over three times as many.

Design and development

When the decision was made to go ahead with a new two-door range, development of the Fintail replacements for the Ponton saloon range was already well advanced. It went without saying that the new two-door models would have to share their mechanical elements with the top-of-the-range Fintail saloons, just as the Ponton two-doors had shared theirs with the top-model Ponton saloons. This time, though, there was a new element in the equation. The two-door Pontons had been essentially 2+2 models, while the extravagant 300S laid claim to be only a two-seater (or three-seater at a pinch). For the new Fintail-based two-doors, Daimler-Benz management

decided that a five-seat capacity would have a much greater appeal. There would therefore be no question of shortening the Fintails' floorpan, which was already designed to suit a five-seater passenger compartment.

In fact, the first sketches for the new two-door models looked little different from the Fintail saloons themselves. They were drawn up in December 1957 by Paul Bracq, a French stylist who had joined Daimler-Benz earlier in the year and who would go on to make his mark on all the new Mercedes models over the next decade (Bracq was subsequently head of styling at BMW and Peugeot as well). Bracq's first designs simply converted the existing saloon design into a two-door pillarless coupé, adding more steeply raked front and rear screens, a noticeably larger dog's-leg cut-out at the leading edge of the doors, a 300SL-style oval 'sports' grille and some larger bumpers. Most of these styling characteristics suggest that he was aiming to please American customers in particular, and it is interesting that the sketches are labelled '300SE' – the top-of-the-range model which would replace the 300S.

However, the design changed quite radically over the next couple of years. Full-size mock-ups built during 1958 still had tail fins, but were otherwise quite close to the eventual production styling and incorporated curved door glasses, which were then at the leading edge of production technology. In addition, the straight lines of the Fintails' lower body had given way to much more distinctive, rounded styling. By 1959, when the first prototypes were built, the tail fins had been pared down to almost nothing.

Launch shots. The 220SE seen on its public debut at the 1961 Geneva Show and airborne during safety testing. With Mercedes' crash testing in its infancy, the engineers were still developing their techniques, hence the makeshift construction of the 'corkscrew' ramp in the background.

minimise production complication and cost. The cabriolet, of course, would need more internal bracing to restore the rigidity which the coupé's fixed steel roof contributed, although the Mercedes engineers were able to keep all the additional metalwork out of sight – mostly in the area around and behind the rear seat – and the structure which went into production was impressively strong and solid-feeling.

In the beginning

The more rounded lines made the bodies rather wider than those of the parent saloons and, although the 2750mm (108.3in) wheelbase remained unchanged and the overall length of 4880mm (192.1in) was within 5mm (0.2in) of the saloons' length, it was hard to recognise in the coupé a derivative of the standard saloon. Only the distinctive *Lichteinheiten*, Mercedes grille (no longer the oval 'sports' type), and Fintail saloon bumpers gave the game away – and before production began, the rear bumper would be changed for a unique style with a longer wrap-round.

The bodyshell and styling of the coupé seem to have been developed first, although Bracq must always have had one eye on the eventual cabriolet derivative because the basic styling had to suit both cars in order to

The first Fintail saloons went on sale during 1959, and no doubt this freed up some engineering resources which could then be devoted to the two-door models. Everything seemed to be in place by September 1960, when the first pilot-production cars – one coupé and one cabriolet, both with the injected 2.2-litre six-cylinder engine – were built at the Sindelfingen works. Full production, however, was still some months away. The first production coupés were built in February 1961 but the first production cabriolets did not come off the lines until September that year.

Meanwhile, the Mercedes range had carried a gap. The fabulous 300S models had actually gone out of production in 1958, and those who hankered after such a prestigious and exclusive car were probably steered gently

The two-door Fintails were a styling triumph for Paul Bracq. The vestigial tail fins – trimmed right down during development – are clear on this 1961 US-market 220SE coupé; this style of number plate lighting was used on US cars. The fuel-injected 2195cc six-cylinder engine is as pristine and correct as the rest of this restored car, although the battery is a modern one with a translucent case – but at least it was supplied by Mercedes!

in the direction of the 300SL roadster during the next couple of years. The 220S Ponton coupés and cabriolets had gone out of production in August 1959, leaving only the more expensive 220SE variants available, and the last of these were made in November 1960. Daimler-Benz was content to leave a further gap before replacing the 300S, but the 220SE had to be replaced as soon as possible. So the first of the new Fintail-based two-doors

to go on sale were 2.2-litre 220SE models. In Mercedes' internal product coding, they were W111 models, like the Fintail 220SE saloons they were based on.

The 220SE coupé was actually unveiled to the press at the re-opening of the Daimler-Benz Museum in Stuttgart during February 1961, an occasion which also celebrated 60 years of the Mercedes name. However, the real public announcement was made at the Geneva Show a month

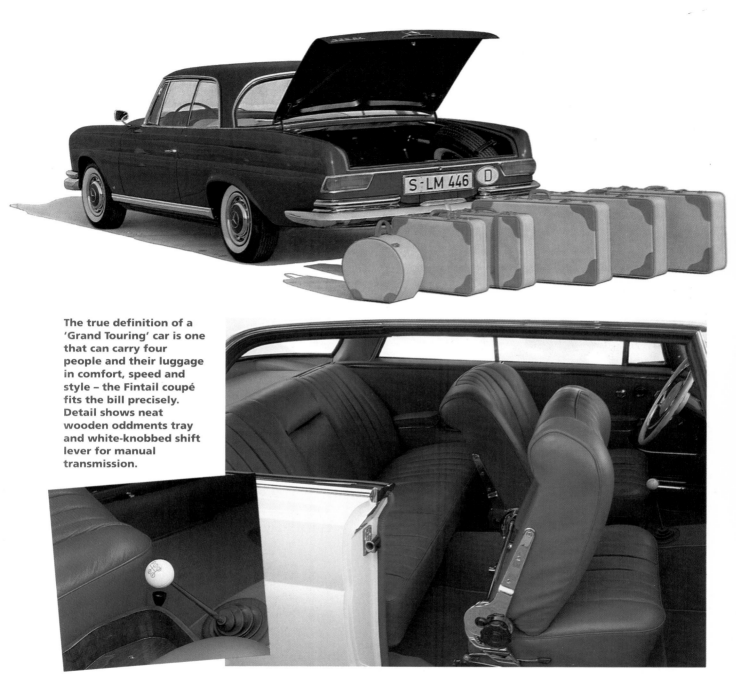

The true definition of a 'Grand Touring' car is one that can carry four people and their luggage in comfort, speed and style – the Fintail coupé fits the bill precisely. Detail shows neat wooden oddments tray and white-knobbed shift lever for manual transmission.

later. There, the new Mercedes vied for star billing with the new E-type Jaguar. It was perhaps unfortunate that only the 220SE coupé was on display; Mercedes would have made an even bigger impact if there had been a cabriolet at Geneva as well, but in fact the company made sure of a second bite at the publicity cherry by holding the open car until the Frankfurt Show in the autumn.

Not that there was any question about the excellence of the two-door models. The fact that their basic styling remained unchanged for 11 years says all that needs to be said about the effectiveness of Paul Bracq's contribution. And the fact that these fabulous motor cars – particularly the cabriolets – are still highly prized possessions nearly a quarter of a century after the last one was built is a clear indication that they are counted among the greatest Mercedes models of the post-1945 era.

Mercedes-Benz Coupés und Cabriolets gelten seit jeher als Meisterwerke der Automobilbaukunst. In diesem Frühjahr setzt die Daimler-Benz AG mit ihrem neuen Mercedes-Benz 220 SE Cabriolet sowie dem Coupé und Cabriolet vom Typ 300 SE diese Tradition fort. Während das 220 SE Cabriolet in seiner technischen Ausstattung dem bereits bekannten Coupé gleicht, ist das 300 SE Cabriolet und Coupé nach der besonderen technischen Konzeption des im Herbst vorigen Jahres vorgestellten Typs 300 SE gestaltet worden. Diese neuen Modelle bilden die Spitze eines Programms, das ebenso anspruchsvolle wie individuelle Wünsche in einem überdurchschnittlichen Maße erfüllt. Die Schönheit, Gediegenheit und sportliche Kraft dieser Fahrzeuge erlaubt es, sie als die Hohe Schule des Automobilbaus zu bezeichnen.

MERCEDES-BENZ
Ihr guter Stern auf allen Straßen

German advert puts 220SE cabriolet to the fore – this car has few rivals from any period in providing such elegant, spacious open-top motoring for four people.

The 220SE

Mechanically, the 220SE two-doors were not quite identical to the 220SE saloons. They shared the same 120PS engine and the same transmission options of four-speed manual or four-speed fluid-coupled automatic, but the two-doors had British-made Girling disc brakes at the front instead of the saloons' finned drums. As the two-door bodies were a lot heavier than their saloon counterparts – the gross weight of the cabriolet was all of 75kg (165lb) more than that of a 220SE saloon – the more powerful brakes were very welcome. Nevertheless, there is little doubt that Daimler-Benz also wanted to present the latest technology on the most expensive model first, and in fact the 220SE saloons took on disc front brakes just a year later.

As far as acceleration and top speed were concerned, the extra weight of the two-door bodies made no discernible difference. Maximum speed was the same 172km/h (107mph) as the saloons boasted, and saloons, cabriolets and coupés alike took around 14secs to reach 100km/h (62mph) from a standing start with the accelerator pressed hard to the floor. These were very respectable figures for the early 1960s, and very similar to those for the much smaller and lighter 190SL roadster. Cars with automatic transmission could feel rather more sluggish than the manual types if left to their own devices, but the manual control of the upshifts which the Mercedes-built gearbox provided allowed the enthusiastic driver of an automatic 220SE to keep up with a well-driven manual car on demanding roads. The two-door models' weight did count against them in one area, though, and that was their steering. Power assistance was an extra-cost option, but it was a brave (or strong) customer who specified a 220SE without it!

While good road manners and above-average performance were important elements in the 220SE two-door package, the real attraction of the cars lay in their distinctive styling and in their luxury fittings. The interior design was masterful, featuring leather upholstery (of course) matched by a polished wooden dashboard. The seats were large and welcoming, and the rear bench offered much more space and comfort than its equivalent on the Ponton 220SE two-doors, even though it was less accommodating than the broad bench of the 220SE Fintail saloon. Headroom in the back was a little restricted, too, and tall passengers had to argue for a place in the front of the car or else slouch rather inelegantly behind. For extra cost, it was possible to order individual rear seats in place of the bench with its folding central armrest, but this option created no more room and remained quite rare.

The general design of the dashboard was similar to the one in the Fintail saloons, although its walnut construction gave it a completely different appearance. Other types of wood could be had to special order – and at a price. The much-criticised 'thermometer' instrument panel of the saloons had also been rejected, and in place of it came a much more sporting layout with two round dials which generally resembled the 300SL panel. One of the dials was, of course, a rev counter, red-lined at 6000rpm, which made its own contribution to the overall aura of high equipment levels and high performance. There was also no shortage of chrome on the dashboard, for these were after all the early 1960s and Mercedes was intending the car to have a strong appeal in the USA, where the fashion for heavy chromework had originated and remained current.

A radio was not standard, but Mercedes recommended a Becker Grand Prix model, which featured the latest self-seeking technology. It also fitted extremely neatly into

Full-size model of a 300SX (right), a landaulet derived from the W111/W112 coupé and dating from the early 1960s; this proposal was not put into production, but a 300SE based on this design was built for Fritz Nallinger. This early 300SE coupé (below) has its gear selector on the steering column and also features the two-tone paint option.

the dashboard, having knobs of the same size and shape as those for the car's other controls and generally looking as if it was built into the design. With it came the electrically-operated telescopic aerial also seen on the 300SE saloon in April 1961, and also in the forefront of technology for the early 1960s. So, too, was the linked wash-wipe for the windscreen, where operation of a button mounted on the toeboard not only sprayed the screen but also triggered the wipers briefly.

Like all open cars, the cabriolets had their own special brand of charm. Bracq's styling ensured that they looked equally good with the top up or down, which is only too often not the case with open cars. Like the Ponton cabriolets which preceded them, they carried their tops in a recess just behind the rear seat, so that only a small amount of fabric and folding mechanism protruded above the bodywork, to be covered by a tightly-fitting bag. On the very first cars, this was made of Alpaca, although leather was later standardised; unfortunately, its relative inflexibility always made fitting the bag something of a chore. The well for the soft-top, of course, took away some of the boot space on cabriolets, although no-one ever complained because there was still plenty of room for luggage: big boots had always been a Mercedes *forte*,

and the one on the coupé was no exception. Perhaps only the absence of power operation for the cabriolet top was a little surprising in view of Mercedes' wish to sell the car in the USA.

These were only the basic specifications. Customers with plenty of money to spend could personalise their 220SEs more or less to their hearts' content. Power-assisted steering, automatic transmission, individual rear seats, different wood on the dashboard and a radio with automatic aerial were just the tip of the iceberg. Also available were an ivory-coloured steering wheel, safety belts, whitewall and radial tyres, electric windows, central door locking, headrests, and a six-piece fitted suitcase set. Coupés could be fitted with a sunroof, and for cars with the column-mounted gearchange option, buyers could order a central front armrest which doubled as a cushion for a third passenger. Naturally, special paint colours were also on the menu, and many coupés were ordered in two-tone schemes, when the roof was generally finished in a darker colour than the lower body.

Throughout their production, the 220SE coupés and cabriolets sold to a fairly wealthy and exclusive clientele. A comparison of prices on the German market makes this abundantly clear. In 1962, a 220SE coupé cost 23,500DM before options were added, and a cabriolet cost 25,500DM. Those figures must be set against just 15,400DM for the top-of-the-range 220SE saloon, and 10,900DM for the entry-level 190 Fintail saloon. When the cars went out of production in 1965, they were still very highly regarded indeed. And the only reason why they went out of production was that Daimler-Benz had developed a new and more powerful 2.5-litre engine to replace the 2.2-litre type in all its forms. It was that engine which went into the existing bodyshells to make the 250SE models.

A 300SE coupé in all its glory. Large round instruments set in polished wood, a steering wheel with central crash pad and plush armchairs characterise the interior of all Fintail coupés and cabriolets, but the day of really lavish use of wood has gone – the dash has a surround of stout padding. By the time this car was built in 1966, American-market models had lost their distinctive twin headlamps and were using the standard *Lichteinheiten*, and the automatic transmission shift is in its later position on the central tunnel.

The 300SE

No matter how up-market they appeared, the 220SE coupés and cabriolets were merely the entry-level models in the Mercedes two-door range. Right from the beginning, Daimler-Benz had planned to build versions with the more powerful 3-litre engine and even higher levels of equipment. These were to wear 300SE badging and were introduced in February 1962 – just a year after the 220SE coupé made its début at the Daimler-Benz Museum in Stuttgart. Some idea of their exclusivity can be gained from their showroom prices in Germany: while a 220SE coupé cost 23,500DM, its 300SE equivalent cost 31,350DM; and while a 220SE cabriolet cost 25,500DM, a 300SE cabriolet was priced at 33,350DM. Whether that price differential of more than 30% was ever justified in terms of value for money is debatable, but around 500 customers a year were prepared to pay it. However, the 300SE always sold in far smaller volumes than the 220SE, the proportion being around five of the smaller-engined cars sold for every one of the larger.

The all-alloy 3-litre engine which lay at the heart of the 300SE coupés and cabriolets had, of course, already been seen in the 300SE saloons in April 1961, and it is described in more detail on pages 40–41. It gave a maximum speed of 180km/h (112mph) with manual transmission in the first 300SE two-doors, which was disappointingly close to the 172km/h (107mph) available from the smaller-engined cars. Not surprisingly, the engine was uprated in January 1964 to give a more respectable 190km/h (118mph) top speed, and customers prepared to sacrifice a little acceleration in return for the

The extra chromework (waistline strip, wheelarch trims) which distinguished 300SE from 220SE is clearly visible on a dark-coloured cabriolet.

ultimate in top speeds could specify taller overall gearing which gave 200km/h (124mph). The popular optional automatic transmission knocked 5km/h (about 3mph) off all these maxima.

Also standard equipment on the two-door 300SE models was the Bosch air suspension from the 300SE saloons, and it was the combination of this and the 3-litre engine which earned the 300SE the same W112 code as its saloon equivalent. However, the 3-litre engine and air suspension were obviously not visible from outside the car, and Mercedes rightly anticipated that buyers who had paid a vast premium for these features wanted to let the owners of lesser 220SE models know the fact! So, as the basic bodyshells of the 300SE two-doors were identical to those on the 220SE two-doors, the 3-litre models had extra chrome to make them distinctive – a full-length trim strip on each flank, and wheelarch highlight strips.

Mercedes made sure not to sell its 300SE customers short in other respects, too. So while the cars' dashboards were generally similar to their 220SE counterparts, they incorporated 220km/h speedometers instead of 210km/h types, and they were generally made of burr walnut rather than plain walnut. The 300SE also featured a courtesy light delay, which kept the interior light on for a few seconds after the doors were closed and was another feature shared with the advanced 300SE saloon.

As already noted, the 300SE was given a power boost in 1964 to improve its top-end performance. However,

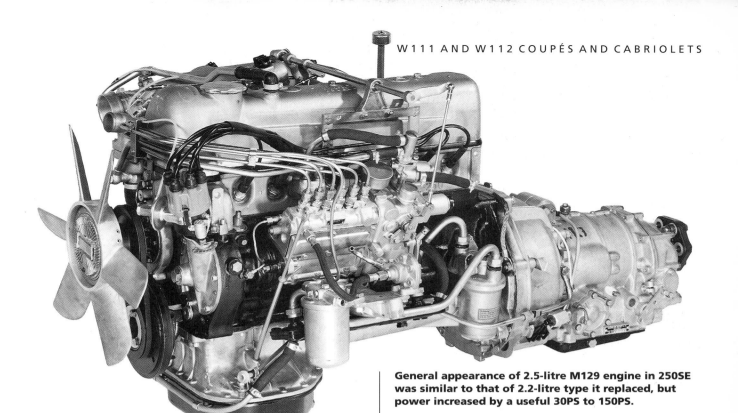

General appearance of 2.5-litre M129 engine in 250SE was similar to that of 2.2-litre type it replaced, but power increased by a useful 30PS to 150PS.

more far-reaching changes were made in the autumn of the following year. The cars picked up the stronger new rear axle designed for the W108 S-class saloons, together with larger disc brakes (made by the German firm of Alfred Teves) and a pressure limiter in the rear brake hydraulic line. To accommodate the larger discs, the Mercedes engineers had to fit 14in wheels in place of the original 13in type, which had the rather unexpected effect of making the car look rather better proportioned than before. The pagoda-roof 230SL, introduced two years earlier, also had 14in wheels, and so the wheel trims fitted to the revised 300SE were simply those already available on the sports car.

Thus revised, the 300SE continued in production until December 1967. By this stage, it was struggling to justify its position as the most expensive of the regular production Mercedes models. Its 3-litre engine offered little more performance than the 2.5-litre engine fitted since 1965 to the 250SE, which had replaced the 220SE coupés and cabriolets, and the new 2.8-litre engine which was just about to replace the 2.5-litre type offered enough performance to make the old 3-litre six-cylinder seem redundant. That the 3-litre engine was noisy at high revs was something which had been apparent for some time, anyway, and was a consequence of its all-alloy construction. In addition, the maladies to which the air

suspension was prone when neglected suggested to Daimler-Benz that this system was perhaps best abandoned. So the 300SE – once the flagship of the Mercedes range – ended its production run on rather a sour note.

The 250SE

The development of W110, W111, W112 variants of the same basic Fintail body design might have made good economic sense to Daimler-Benz, but it did not go down too well with customers of the more expensive saloons. Buyers of a Fintail 300SE were not amused to discover how closely their cars resembled a 190D taxi, and by the early 1960s it was clear that Mercedes really needed a distinctive saloon bodyshell for its upmarket models.

Paul Bracq's early attempts to style such a saloon were heavily derivative of his design for the two-door coupés, and in fact the earliest full-size model was little more than a four-door version of the coupé! That evolved in due course into the rather more angular style of the W108 and W109 S-class cars which were introduced in 1965, by which time there were concerns about how well the styling of the two-door models was wearing. So in March 1965, Bracq put forward a new coupé design proposal, this time bringing the wheel full circle and basing his two-door style on the production styling of the S-class saloons. Pictures make clear that the style would have

dated quickly and it was not adopted for production.

In styling terms, the new S-class cars therefore did not affect the cabriolets and coupés. In mechanical terms, however, they did. It was their new and stronger rear axle which went into the revised 300SE in 1965, and it was their new 2.5-litre engine which replaced the 2.2-litre engine in the 220SE cabriolets and coupés to turn them into 250SE models in September 1965.

The 2.2-litre engine, of course, was an elderly design by this date, having been introduced as long ago as 1951.

With such a short production life, the 250SE is highly desirable these days – and especially rare in right-hand drive form. This one has automatic transmission.

In 1963, it was bored out to give 2.3 litres for the 230SL sports car, and for the S-class saloons it was further developed with a long stroke and seven main bearings instead of four to give 2.5 litres (2496cc). The 2.3-litre M127 engine also saw service in the Fintail 230 and 230S models, while the injected version of the 2.5-litre M129

The last versions of the W111 cabriolets and coupés were powered by Mercedes' new 3.5-litre V8 engine. Production ended in 1971. There was also a 2.8-litre six-cylinder car after the 250SE bowed out in 1967. This example has incorrect wheelarch trims.

was a natural choice to replace the 2.2-litre engine in the prestigious coupés and cabriolets.

The 2.5-litre engine offered 150PS, which represented a healthy increase over the 120PS of the 2.2-litre type and gave the 250SE coupés and cabriolets a maximum speed of 193km/h (120mph) with manual transmission. This was 300SE territory. The 250SE models had the same 14in wheels as the revised 300SE types and, air suspension and chrome decoration apart, there was not a lot to distinguish the dearer models from the cheaper ones.

However, the 250SE two-doors were not an unqualified success. The 2.5-litre engine may have offered more power and torque than the 2.2-litre type, but it was noticeably more thirsty. For that very reason, the 250SE models had the 82-litre fuel tank introduced on the 300SE models in January 1963 rather than the 65-litre type of the 220SE and earlier 300SE. The 2.5-litre engine was also prone to a number of problems and quickly

gained a fairly negative reputation. Early examples drank oil and cars of all ages developed noisy valve gear, so it was not uncommon for one of these engines to need a major overhaul at 100,000km (62,000 miles) – which was very early indeed by Mercedes standards. So work began on an entirely new six-cylinder engine, and the twin overhead camshaft 2.8-litre M130 was rushed into production as soon as Mercedes was able.

For that reason, the 250SE cabriolets and coupés lasted in production only until December 1967. Production averaged out at just over 2000 examples a year, which was rather less than the 220SE types had achieved. Of course, it was true that the styling of the two-door models was no longer new, and it is arguable that this contributed to declining sales in a market where fashion is vitally important. However, it is also true that sales of the two-door models picked up again later, after the 2.5-litre engine had been dropped – which makes fairly clear where the problem lay.

Nevertheless, a 250SE coupé or cabriolet today is still a highly desirable car. In a collector's world where rarity has its own value, this rarest of the two-door W111 Mercedes remains interesting alongside the generally better-equipped 300SE and the more widely liked 220SE.

COMPETITION

During the early 1950s, the Mercedes-Benz competitions department was wholly focused on Grand Prix racing and on long-distance events for sports racing cars. Its efforts were enormously successful, and the W196 Grand Prix cars and 300SLR sports racers captured for Mercedes both the World Championship at the Grand Prix circuits and the Sports Car Constructors' Championship during the 1955 season. However, that season certainly left a sour taste in the mouths of those who worked for the Mercedes competitions department, because a tragic accident involving a 300SLR during the Le Mans 24-hour race had killed driver Pierre Levegh and more than 80 spectators. For 1956, Mercedes switched from the high-profile glamour of the tracks and

Possibly the best ever rallying moment for Mercedes. The 1960 Monte Carlo Rally was a massive triumph for the 'works' team, which carried off the first three places and the Manufacturer's Team prize. This was the first appearance of the brand new Fintail 220SE models, and all of them ran in the traditional Mercedes racing silver. In first place were Walter Schock and Rolf Moll, seen roaring up a mountain incline on their way to victory.

road racing to low-profile entries in saloon car events.

The Ponton 180 and its diesel equivalent had always been too slow to have any real interest as competition cars. However, the 220 announced in 1954 was a very different matter. Rugged like the 180, but much faster

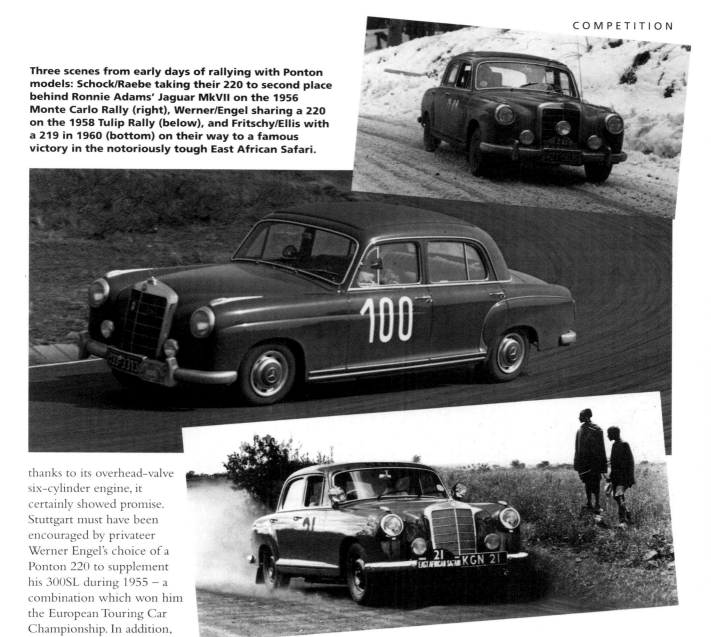

Three scenes from early days of rallying with Ponton models: Schock/Raebe taking their 220 to second place behind Ronnie Adams' Jaguar MkVII on the 1956 Monte Carlo Rally (right), Werner/Engel sharing a 220 on the 1958 Tulip Rally (below), and Fritschy/Ellis with a 219 in 1960 (bottom) on their way to a famous victory in the notoriously tough East African Safari.

thanks to its overhead-valve six-cylinder engine, it certainly showed promise. Stuttgart must have been encouraged by privateer Werner Engel's choice of a Ponton 220 to supplement his 300SL during 1955 – a combination which won him the European Touring Car Championship. In addition, Mercedes 220s that year claimed third and fifth positions overall on the Monte Carlo Rally, driven respectively by H. Gerdum/J. Kuhling and Walter Schock/Rolf Moll.

So from 1956 works support was made available to selected drivers who entered the major races and rallies with production Mercedes saloons. Schock once again did well in the Monte, this time with co-driver K. Raebe, when his 'works' 220 finished second overall and won its class. And over the next two years Pontons claimed minor trophies in a variety of events, often in the hands of privateer Eugen Böhringer – who would later become a major force behind the wheel of a Mercedes saloon.

While it soon became clear that the 220 was too heavy and unwieldy ever to make it to the top of the heap, the 219 was a different matter. Introduced in 1956, it was both lighter and more agile than the 220, and before long it became the favoured mount of those who used Mercedes saloons in competition. Its most spectacular achievements were first places in the 1959 and 1960 East African Safari Rallies, in each case driven by Bill Fritschy and Jack Ellis. By 1960, however, the focus of works support was changing because the new Fintail models had entered production, so the 219's competition career was cut rather short.

The four-cylinder cars also enjoyed some success in

Contrasting fortunes on the Monte. Second place in the remarkable 1-2-3 team performance of 1960 (left) went to Eugen Böhringer, whose car had already suffered some damage when this shot was taken in the mountains above Nice; protective wire mesh headlamp covers are clearly visible. Damage of a different kind (below left), a drunken front wheel, is seen on Böhringer's car on the Grand Prix circuit in the 1961 event, where a strange handicapping system made Panhards the unlikely winners. Note that the cars carry the same S-JX 74 registration.

the later 1950s. During 1959, for example, a 190 driven by Paulsen and Sommens took first place in the minor-league Winter Rally in South Africa. Even the 190D received some exposure and works support, and a car driven by competitions department manager and former racing driver Karl Kling with Rainer Günzler won its class in the 1959 Algiers-Capetown Rally.

Mercedes' support for the Pontons in competition always seemed rather patchy, but the company resolved to do the job properly with the new Fintail saloons. The chosen weapon was the 220SE, backed up during the 1963 and 1964 seasons by the 300SE. There were no more works entries after 1964 (although Manfred Schiek did campaign a 230bhp 300SE during 1965), but early in

the 1960s Mercedes saloons won no fewer than three European Rally Championships. The 220SE became *the* car to beat in rallies and road races, although it was never promoted seriously as a circuit racer.

Mercedes were taking no chances when they entered a team of three 220SE models in the 1960 Monte Carlo Rally. It was meticulous preparation which had led to the company's domination of Grand Prix racing in the 1930s and the early 1950s, and similar effort went into the Monte as all three crews spent between six and eight weeks practising the 175-mile Mountain Circuit around Monte Carlo that Stuttgart believed would decide the rally. The result totally justified the considerable preparation: the 220SEs finished first, second and third

Two track scenes with 220SE models: during the 1960 Nürburgring Six Hours (right) Golderer's car pauses in the pits for refuelling, while in the 1961 Polish Rally (below) Böhringer heads for victory in an unfamiliar partnership with Finnish driver Rauno Aaltonen – who went on to become one of rallying's 'greats'.

overall, and carried off the Manufacturers' team prize. The winning team of Schock/Moll lost only 30secs on the Mountain Circuit, while second-placed Eugen Böhringer (partnered by H. Socher) lost just 1min 48secs. The highest-placed non-Mercedes entry was Peter Harper's Sunbeam Rapier, which lost nearly 11mins! Third overall was the works partnership of Ott/Mahle, while fifth – behind Harper's Sunbeam – was *another* 220SE, this time the privately-entered car of Tak/Swaab.

This Monte success started off an excellent year for the 220SEs, and particularly for Schock/Moll. They took first places in the Polish and Acropolis Rallies, second in the Viking Rally, third in the Tulip Rally, fourth in the German Rally and fifth in the Geneva Rally – a string of successes which earned them the European Touring Car Championship for 1960.

However, 1961 was not to be such a good year. A controversial new handicap system in the Monte Carlo Rally put the 220SEs out of contention (the tiny French Panhards were the unlikely winners), but the cars did do well in other events. Works 220SEs took first and second places in no fewer than three major events, these being the Central African Rally (Karl Kling/Rainer Günzler and Bettoja/Eger), the East African Safari Rally (Manussis/Coleridge/Beckett and

Four great victories were achieved in 1962, when the 220SE had become firmly established as the top rallying saloon, and here is a scene from each. Three of these successes went to ace driver Böhringer, seen with S-JX 71 and victory spoils after the Acropolis (above) and Liège-Sofia-Liège (above right), and in action on the Polish (right). The other significant moment came when Swedish lady drivers Ewy Rosqvist and Ursula Wirth (below) won the Argentine Touring Car Race.

Although the 'works' effort for 1963 concentrated on the 300SE, lesser models still took part in rallies that year. Dieter Glemser (right), later to become a saloon racing star in the 1970s, won the Polish Rally in a 220SE, while a four-cylinder Fintail (below), a type that never figured in the 'works' campaigns, is seen on the Monte, where these privateer entrants were possibly encouraged to try their luck because of new handicap regulations that favoured smaller-engined cars.

Fritschy/Mandeville) and the Argentine Touring Car Rally (Schock/Schiek and Herrmann/Günzler).

The following season, 1962, was the year of Eugen Böhringer, who won back the European Touring Car Championship for Mercedes with his works-prepared 220SE. Böhringer's astonishing string of successes that year consisted of first places in the Acropolis, Polish and Liège-Sofia-Liège Rallies, second places in the German and Monte Carlo Rallies, fifth in the Midnight Sun Rally and seventh in the Tulip Rally. Other works 220SEs won the Argentine Touring Car Rally (Ewy Rosqvist/Ursula Wirth) and the Tour d'Europe (Rudi Golderer/Becker), while privateer Rolf Kreder won the German Rally Championship with his own 220SE.

For 1963, Böhringer switched to the 300SE, which

that year made its debut as a works rally car. Although he drove the new 230SL sports model in the Spa-Sofia-Liège Rally, it was the 300SE which took him to first places in the Acropolis Rally and in the Argentine Touring Car Race, and the aggregate of all his results that year made him European Rally Champion for the second year running. Other 300SEs did well in the Acropolis Rally, where they won the Team Prize for Mercedes, and in the Argentine Touring Car Rally, where second place went to Glemser/Braungart and fourth to Bordeu/Winter.

Meanwhile, the 220SEs continued to perform well. Glemser/Braungart took their 220SE to first place in the Polish Rally and second in the German Rally, while Rosqvist/Wirth won a *Coupe des Dames* in the Monte Carlo Rally and came third among the 300SEs in the Argentine Touring Car Race.

But things were getting tougher. BMC had started to campaign the Mini Cooper S and Ford's British arm had introduced the Cortina GT, while the American parent company were using Falcons in Europe. Böhringer did his best with a 220SE in the Monte that year, but without result, and the 220SE which Ewy Rosqvist-Korff (who had retained her maiden name on marriage) and Manfred Schiek took to sixth overall in the Spa-Sofia-Liège Rally was running a prototype 2.5-litre engine.

The works 300SEs were now running on 15in wheels to improve their ground clearance and had five-speed ZF

The year of the 300SE, and a swan song for Mercedes in top-level rallying: 1963 was another highly successful season, and Eugen Böhringer once again proved to be the dominant 'works' driver. Here he is on three victorious outings, blasting across the finish line in the Argentine Touring Car Race (top), taking a break on the Acropolis (above) and looking relaxed at the wheel in the Nürburgring Six Hours (above right).

gearboxes, while their engines were tuned to 195PS at the beginning of the season and were pumping out 205PS by its end. Partnered by Erich Waxenberger, Böhringer drove his 300SE to second place in the Swedish Kanonlöppet Rally. He also won the Argentine Touring Car Race with

Kaiser in the navigator's seat, but was denied a place in the Spa-Francorchamps 24-hour race through an unfortunate disqualification. The Spa-Francorchamps event nevertheless did fall to a 300SE, driven by the Belgian pair of Crevits and Gosselin.

But the writing was on the wall by this stage. A new generation of smaller and nimbler cars was taking over from the big and powerful rally cars of the late 1950s and early 1960s, and the Fintail saloons could not be kept competitive. So Mercedes did not run a works team for the 1965 season, preferring instead to leave the formidable record of the 220SE and 300SE rally cars to remain unblemished.

LIVING ON

These Mercedes-Benz motor cars were built to last, and the quality of their construction and of the engineering which went into them was such that large numbers have survived through to the present day. It would be fair to say that the majority of those that have survived now lead rather easier lives than they did when they were new, generally as the pampered pets of enthusiast owners. However, small numbers are still in everyday use, and in some African and Middle Eastern countries an elderly Mercedes – even one *this* elderly – is a status symbol of sorts.

The Ponton saloons, Fintail saloons and their two-door derivatives were built at a time when Mercedes was expanding its distribution network into new territories. Among those, the USA became the most important in terms of sales volume, although it took some time for the saloons to make the sort of impact which the 300SL and 190SL sports cars had made in the first half of the 1950s.

It was this image of Mercedes as a high-quality and high-priced import that dictated which cars would be most successful in the USA: buyers took to the cabriolets and coupés, and they took to the more expensive six-cylinder saloons. Four-cylinder models, however, were never strong sellers in that country.

That contrasted, of course, with the position in many African countries, where the rugged four-cylinder models were the best-sellers and the six-cylinders were generally too expensive for all but the very wealthy (which in practice usually meant Government authorities). In continental Europe and in Germany itself, the contrast between six-cylinder and four-cylinder sales was less marked. Countries like France, however, probably took more four-cylinders than six-cylinders simply because of their taxation system which penalised the drivers of powerful big-engined cars. In Britain, punitive import taxes meant that the four-cylinder Mercedes were poor

Mercedes cars have a deserved reputation for exceptional durability, but they are not indestructible. The car in the foreground of this graveyard scene is a later model (note the full-width bonnet air vent), but a four-cylinder Fintail wreck languishes behind.

value when compared to domestic products, and so it was the six-cylinder cars which sold better, and then mostly to the wealthy – which inevitably limited their numbers.

People who want to buy an older Mercedes often imagine that the process is a combination of fun and profit. It should most certainly always be fun, but the profit element needs careful consideration. Keeping an elderly Mercedes up to scratch can be a very expensive business, especially if major structural restoration work is needed somewhere along the line, and relatively few of the cars are likely to increase in value significantly. Frankly, the sensible way to approach ownership is with the assumption that while an elderly Mercedes will not lose its value in the way that a modern car does, it is also unlikely to increase in value. Whatever it costs to keep it running is best seen as the cost of keeping the car as a hobby, and not as something to be recouped in an eventual sale.

There are exceptions to this general rule, of course, and some of the cars covered in this book certainly can be seen as investments of a kind. Inevitably, these are the rarer and more exotic types, and equally inevitably they are the ones which will cost more to buy in the first place. Starting at the top, the 220SE, 250SE and 300SE cabriolets built between 1961-67 are undoubtedly the models with the best investment potential. Even 30 years after they were built, their imposing appearance has hardly dated, and the fact that they are open cars gives them enormous appeal. Running rather behind them are

the coupé versions, which have a slightly greater practical appeal but rather less glamour.

At about the same level as the Fintail-derived coupés are the Ponton-based cabriolets, and of course the coupé versions of those come next in line. There is, then, quite a gap in prices before the saloons come into the picture. Most desirable here are the 300SE (especially in fully-loaded, long-wheelbase form), the 220SE Fintail and the 220SE Ponton. Other six-cylinders trail some way behind, and cannot really be seen as investments. The four-cylinders and diesels are strictly for enthusiasts only. In fact, the only four-cylinders or diesels which really have any significant value at all are likely to be very low-mileage examples in immaculate original condition – the sort of cars which have to be kept in a heated garage to retain their value and cannot really be used and enjoyed.

Most real enthusiasts are more concerned with the practicalities of ownership rather than the investment potential, however, and rather different criteria apply here. The desirability ratings suggested above can probably be reversed, because while a four-cylinder car with basic equipment may be kept on the road relatively cheaply, the cost of repairs to the air suspension of a 300SE, to the fuel injection of any one of the more expensive models, or to the interior of a cabriolet or coupé can be enough to deter all but the most dedicated (or wealthy) enthusiast. The diesel models have their own charm and period interest, but they are most definitely not cars to use regularly in modern cut-and-thrust traffic because they

Cloth interiors (right) rarely survive this well, the fabric commonly wearing thin and then falling apart; MB-Tex rexine upholstery is more durable, but its stitched seams give way. Trim items like this 'dowager strap' (below) in an early Ponton saloon are not as resilient as they might be, and sometimes difficult to replace. Identification plates (below right) explain the exact age and specification of a car; these examples are on the front inner wing of a Ponton saloon.

are slow and rather cumbersome. Ambulances, estate cars and other conversions have their own devotees, but their relative rarity has not resulted in increased desirability or in higher values, so these vehicles are best seen as interesting curiosities.

Mercedes owners are far better served than the owners of most other classic cars. Mercedes itself provides very valuable support through its classic division, but that support is expensive. Items like bumpers and rear lamps for the Fintail-based two-doors are priced out of all proportion to similar items for modern Mercedes – and even those are costly enough. Body parts for the low-volume two-door Ponton models are also frighteningly expensive – when available. However, there are plenty of specialists who supply remanufactured panels for the more lowly saloons, particularly in Germany, and these are not prohibitively expensive. Much more problematical in general are likely to be smaller items, such as chromed

window frames for the two-door Fintails, or original steering wheels and switchgear. The good news is that, once in good condition structurally, these cars are not likely to deteriorate quickly. Repairs can therefore be viewed quite legitimately as an investment in a car's future, as long as they are carried out properly. It is never worth trying to get work done 'on the cheap', though, because poor quality is likely to show eventually.

Interior trim and fittings are generally durable, although the original woolcloth upholstery found on so many cars does eventually wear into holes. Far more durable is the MB-Tex rexine alternative. The optional leather upholstery is also very durable, although like all leather it is prone to fading, drying out and then cracking. Large-scale replacement can be very expensive. The wood trim on the more expensive models is also very hard-wearing, much more so than in most British cars of a similar vintage. However, it does suffer badly when exposed to strong sunlight, and the garnish rail at the bottom of the windscreen on Fintail-based cabriolets (so often used in sunny weather!) is particularly prone to deterioration. Refinishing it to the original standard is a job best left to experts.

The mechanical elements of these cars are formidably durable. Gearboxes almost never give trouble, although the column change mechanism can become sloppy. Clutches, particularly on Ponton models, are not particularly long-lived, and the clutch friction lining is likely to need even more frequent replacement on cars fitted with the rare Hydrak clutch – which is very much a mixed blessing.

Most of the engines will manage 400,000km (250,000 miles) without major work if they are properly looked after. However, those cars with Solex carburettors are notoriously poor starters, and many owners have gone for a Weber conversion. Parts in general are not a problem, but some of the less commonly needed items can sometimes be difficult to obtain. It is worth noting in this context that there are often several different versions of what appears at first sight to be the same engine. There were, for example, two different versions of the M121 1.9-litre four-cylinder petrol engine in the Ponton 190, a third in the final Ponton 180, a fourth in the Fintail 190 and yet a fifth in the 190SL sports car. Parts which will suit one version of the engine are not guaranteed to suit another, and it is always worth remembering that the engine fitted to any given car might not be the correct type if an earlier owner has fitted a replacement.

A word of caution is needed about the 3-litre and 2.5-litre six-cylinder engines. The 3-litre is fundamentally a reliable engine in the best Mercedes tradition, but its all-alloy construction makes it a little more delicate than the iron-block engines. Waterway corrosion with resultant overheating can be a problem, and repairs are likely to be expensive. Finding some parts for this engine can also be difficult. The 2.5-litre engine was one of Mercedes' least successful designs, and was prone when new to big-end bearing and centre main bearing troubles. Modifications can be made today to prevent these troubles, but their cost is always worth investigating before purchasing a car with an unmodified engine.

Fuel injection systems have an unwarranted reputation for problems. Uneven running and other troubles are most often caused by nothing worse than incorrect maintenance. The Bosch mechanical injection systems are not easy to set up properly, and do need the attention of an expert who understands them; fuel injection specialists are not necessarily the people to trust, as their expertise is most commonly focused on the more modern electronic injection systems. It is rare for a major component like the injection pump to need replacement, which is very fortunate because such items are very expensive.

Suspension problems are more common, particularly at the front end when regular greasing of the king-pins has not been carried out. Parts are available, however, and most problems can be fairly readily – though again not inexpensively – put right. At the back of the cars, the different varieties of swing-axle suspension are much of a muchness for durability, but the radius arms can pull out of the floorpan. The air suspension on 300SE models is a very different matter. Never wholly satisfactory when new, principally because of rigorous maintenance requirements, it is prone to leaking valves which will cause a car to sink down overnight (or in bad cases, even more quickly) when the pressure pump is not being driven by the engine. The pump itself is another very expensive item to replace, and there are parts availability problems for the system as a whole which make a major overhaul something to be dreaded.

This is not the place to provide a full list of all the owners' clubs which cater for the Ponton and Fintail models world-wide, because contact addresses change from time to time and such a list would rapidly become out of date. However, there are Mercedes-Benz clubs in all the cars' major Western market territories, and their current addresses can be found easily enough through the classic car magazines. Joining one of these clubs is very worthwhile indeed for the classic Mercedes owner, if only because contact with other enthusiasts who run the same type of car can provide valuable information and experience which is difficult to find anywhere else. Fellow enthusiasts are also likely to have experience of the various specialist repairers and parts suppliers, and will be able to recommend good ones (and, conversely, warn about poor ones).

Owning a classic Mercedes-Benz saloon, cabriolet or coupé from the 1950s or 1960s can be an immensely enjoyable experience, but it is important to remember that the cars were built to be used and that fewer problems are likely to arise if they do get used regularly. Much of the fun in ownership comes from driving the car, from attracting the interest of non-enthusiasts, and from being able to arouse their interest further by sharing one's own enthusiasm and experiences. That simply cannot happen if a car is kept in a heated garage all the time and is never taken out to be driven and admired by those who remember them fondly, or have never even seen one before.

APPENDIX

Technical specifications

W120 models: 180 (1953–57), 180a (1957–59), 180b (1959–61), 180c (1961–62) Engine Type M136 in-line four-cylinder petrol (1953–57), type M121 in-line four-cylinder petrol (1957–62) **Crankshaft** Three main bearings **Bore × stroke** 75mm × 100mm (1953–57), 85mm × 83.6mm (1957–62) **Capacity** 1767cc (1953–57), 1897cc (1957–62) **Valves** Side inlet and side exhaust valves (1953–57), overhead camshaft (1957–62) **Compression ratio** 6.8:1 **Fuel system** Solex 32 PICB carburettor (1953–59), Solex 34PICB carburettor (1959–62) **Maximum power** 52PS at 4000rpm (1953–57), 65PS at 4500rpm (1957–59), 68PS at 4400rpm (1959–62) **Maximum torque** 11.4mkg (82.5lb ft) at 1800rpm (1953–57), 13mkg (94lb ft) at 2200rpm (1957–59), 13.2mkg (96lb ft) at 2500rpm (1959–62) **Transmission** Four-speed all-synchromesh gearbox; ratios 4.05:1, 2.38:1, 1.53:1, 1.00:1, reverse 3.92:1 **Final drive** 3.89:1 (1953–57), 3.90:1 (1957–62) **Brakes** Hydraulic drum front and rear; mechanical handbrake on rear wheels; vacuum servo optional from 1959 **Front suspension** Independent, with unequal-length wishbones and coil springs **Rear suspension** Swing-axle type, with coil springs (single-pivot swing-axles from Sep 1955) **Steering** Recirculating ball, with 18.5:1 ratio **Wheels and tyres** 13in wheels with 6.40-13 tyres **Length** 4485mm (176.4in) **Wheelbase** 2650mm (104.3in) **Width** 1740mm (68.5in) **Height** 1560mm (61.4in) **Front track** 1430mm (55.9in) **Rear track** 1475mm (58.1in) **Unladen weight** 1180kg (2601lb) 1953–55, 1200kg (2645lb) 1955–57, 1210kg (2667lb) 1957–62 **Gross vehicle weight** 1600kg (3527lb) 1953–55, 1615kg (3560lb) 1955–62 **Top speed** 126km/h (78.29mph) 1953–57, 136km/h (84.5mph) 1957–62 **0-100km/h** (0-62mph) 31sec (1953–57), 21sec (1957–62)

W120 models: 180D (1954–59), 180Db (1959–61), 180Dc (1961–62) As contemporary petrol-engined 180, except: **Engine** Type OM636 in-line four-cylinder indirect injection diesel (1954–61), type OM621 in-line four-cylinder indirect injection diesel (1961–62) **Crankshaft** Three main bearings **Bore × stroke** 75mm × 100mm (1954–61), 87mm × 83.6mm (1961–62) **Capacity** 1767cc (1954–61), 1897cc (1961–62) **Valves** Pushrod-operated overhead valves (1954–61), overhead camshaft (1961–62) **Compression ratio** 19:1 (1954–61), 21:1 (1961–62) **Fuel system** Bosch injection pump **Maximum power** 40PS at 3200rpm (1954–55), 43PS at 3500rpm (1955–61), 48PS at 3800rpm (1961–62) **Maximum torque** 10.3mkg (75lb ft) at 2000rpm (1954–61), 11.0mkg (80lb ft) at 2200rpm (1961–62) **Final drive** 3.7:1 **Brakes** Greater swept area (1957–62) **Unladen weight** 1220kg (2689lb) **Gross vehicle weight** 1650kg (3637lb) 1953–55, 1660kg (3660lb) 1961–62 **Top speed** 112km/h (69.59mph) 1953–55, 115km/h (71.46mph) 1955–61, 120km/h (74.56mph) 1961–62 **0-100km/h** (0-62mph) 39sec (1953–55), 37sec (1955–61), 36sec (1961–62)

W121 models: 190 (1956–59), 190b (1959–61) As for contemporary petrol-engined 180, except: **Engine** Type M121 in-line four-cylinder petrol **Crankshaft** Three main bearings **Bore × stroke** 85mm × 83.6mm **Capacity** 1897cc **Valves** Overhead camshaft **Compression ratio** 7.5:1 (1956–59), 8.5:1 (1959–61) **Fuel system** Solex 32 PAITA carburettor **Maximum power** 75PS at 4600rpm (1956–59), 80PS at 4800rpm (1959–61) **Maximum torque** 13.9mkg (101lb ft) at 2800rpm (1956–59), 14.2mkg (103lb ft) at 2800rpm (1959–61) **Final drive** 4.1:1 **Brakes** Greater swept area (as 180b) and optional vacuum servo assistance **Rear suspension** Single-pivot swing-axles **Length** 4500mm (177.2in) from 1959 **Unladen weight** 1240kg (2733lb) **Gross vehicle weight** 1650kg (3637lb) **Top speed** 139km/h (86.37mph) 1956–59, 144km/h (89.48mph) 1959–61 **0-100km/h** (0-62mph) 20.5sec (1956–59), 19sec (1959–61)

W121 models: 190D (1958–59), 190Db (1959–61) As for contemporary petrol-engined 190, except: **Engine** Type OM621 in-line four-cylinder indirect-injection diesel **Crankshaft** Three main bearings

Bore × stroke 85mm × 83.6mm **Capacity** 1897cc **Valves** Overhead camshaft **Compression ratio** 21:1 **Fuel system** Bosch injection pump **Maximum power** 50PS at 4000rpm **Maximum torque** 11mkg (79.5lb ft) at 2200rpm **Final drive** 3.7:1 **Brakes** No servo option **Unladen weight** 1250kg (2755lb) **Gross vehicle weight** 1660kg (3659lb) **Top speed** 126km/h (78.29mph) **0-100km/h** (0-62mph) 29sec

W105 models: 219 (1956–59) Engine Type M180 in-line six-cylinder **Crankshaft** Four main bearings **Bore × stroke** 80mm × 72.8mm **Capacity** 2195cc **Valves** Overhead camshaft **Compression ratio** 7.6:1 (1956–57), 8.7:1 (1957–59) **Fuel system** Solex 32 PAATJ dual-choke carburettor **Maximum power** 85PS at 4800rpm (1956–57), 90PS at 4800rpm (1957–59) **Maximum torque** 16mkg (116lb ft) at 2400rpm (1956–57), 17mkg (123lb ft) at 2400rpm (1957–59) **Transmission** Four-speed all-synchromesh gearbox; ratios 3.52:1, 2.32:1, 1.52:1, 1.00:1, reverse 3.29:1; optional Hydrak automatic clutch (1957–59) **Final drive** 4.1:1 (1956–57), 3.9:1 (1957–59) **Brakes** Hydraulic drum front and rear; mechanical handbrake on rear wheels; optional servo assistance **Front suspension** Independent, with coil springs **Rear suspension** Single-pivot swing-axles with coil springs **Steering** Recirculating ball, with 21.4:1 ratio **Wheels and tyres** 13in wheels with 6.40-13 tyres **Length** 4680mm (184.3in) **Wheelbase** 2750mm (108.3in) **Width** 1740mm (68.5in) **Height** 1560mm (61.4in) **Front track** 1430mm (56.3in) **Rear track** 1470mm (57.9in) **Unladen weight** 1290kg (2844lb) **Gross vehicle weight** 1710kg (3770lb) **Top speed** 148km/h (92mph) **0-100km/h** (0-62mph) 17sec

W180 saloon models: 220 (1954–56), 220S (1956–59) Engine Type M180 in-line six-cylinder **Crankshaft** Four main bearings **Bore × stroke** 80mm × 72.8mm **Capacity** 2195cc **Valves** Overhead camshaft **Compression ratio** 7.6:1 **Fuel system** Solex 32 PAATJ dual-choke carburettor (220), two Solex 32 PAJTA carburettors (220S) **Maximum power** 85PS at 4800rpm (220), 100PS at 4800rpm (220S, 1956–57), 106PS at 5200rpm (220S, 1957–59) **Maximum torque** 16mkg (116lb ft) at 2400rpm (220), 16.5mkg (119lb ft) at 3500rpm (220S, 1956–57), 17.5 mkg (127lb ft) at 3500rpm (220S, 1957–59) **Transmission** Four-speed all-synchromesh gearbox; ratios 3.40:1 (3.52:1 for later 220 and all 220S), 2.32:1, 1.52:1, 1.00:1, reverse 3.29:1; optional Hydrak automatic clutch (220S, 1957–59) **Final drive** 4.11:1 (early 220), 4.10:1 (later 220 and all 220S) **Brakes** Hydraulic drum front and rear; mechanical handbrake on rear wheels; servo assistance on 220 (1955–59) and on all 220S **Front suspension** Independent, with coil springs **Rear suspension** Single-pivot swing-axles with coil springs **Steering** Recirculating ball, with 21.4:1 ratio **Wheels and tyres** 13in wheels with 6.70-13 tyres **Length** 4715mm (187in) **Wheelbase** 2820mm (111in) **Width** 1740mm (68.5in) **Height** 1560mm (61.4in) **Front track** 1430mm (56.3in) **Rear track** 1470mm (57.9in) **Unladen weight** 1300kg (2866lb), 220; 1350kg (2976lb), 220S **Gross vehicle weight** 1730kg (3814lb), 220; 1790kg (3946lb), 220S **Top speed** 150km/h (93.2mph), 220; 160km/h (99.42mph), 220S **0-100km/h** (0-62mph) 19sec (220), 17sec (220S)

W180 cabriolets and coupés: 220S (1956–59) As for contemporary W180 220S saloon, except: **Engine** Type M180 in-line six-cylinder **Crankshaft** Four main bearings **Bore × stroke** 80mm × 72.8mm **Capacity** 2195cc **Valves** Overhead camshaft **Compression ratio** 7.6:1 (1956–57), 8.7:1 (1957–59) **Fuel system** Two Solex 32 PAJTA carburettors **Maximum power** 100PS at 4800rpm (1956–57), 106PS at 5200rpm (1957–59) **Maximum torque** 16.5mkg (119lb ft) at 3500rpm (1956–57), 17.5mkg (127lb ft) at 3500rpm (1957–59) **Length** 4670mm (183.9in) **Wheelbase** 2700mm (106.3in) **Width** 1765mm (69.5in) **Height** 1530mm (60.2in) **Front track** 1430mm (56.3in) **Rear track** 1470mm (57.9in) **Unladen weight** 1410kg (3108lb), Coupé; 1450kg (3196lb), Cabriolet **Gross vehicle weight** 1815kg (4001lb) **Top speed** 160km/h (99.42mph) **0-100km/h** (0-62mph) 17sec

W128 saloon models: 220SE (1958–59) Engine Type M127 in-line six-cylinder **Crankshaft** Four main bearings **Bore × stroke** 80mm × 72.8mm **Capacity** 2195cc **Valves** Overhead camshaft **Compression ratio** 8.7:1 **Fuel system** Bosch fuel injection, with twin-piston pump **Maximum power** 115PS at 4800rpm **Maximum torque** 19mkg (152lb ft) at 4100rpm **Transmission** Four-speed all-synchromesh gearbox; ratios 3.52:1, 2.32:1, 1.52:1, 1.00:1, reverse 3.29:1. US models only: 3.65:1, 2.36:1, 1.53:1, 1.00:1, reverse 3.29:1; optional Hydrak automatic clutch **Final drive** 4.1:1 **Brakes** Hydraulic drum front and rear, with servo assistance; mechanical handbrake on rear wheels **Front suspension** Independent, with coil springs **Rear suspension** Single-pivot swing-axles with coil springs **Steering** Recirculating ball, with 21.4:1 ratio **Wheels and tyres** 13in wheels with 6.70-13 tyres **Length** 4750mm (187in) **Wheelbase** 2820mm (111in) **Width** 1740mm (68.5in) **Height** 1560mm (61.4in) **Front track** 1430mm (56.3in) **Rear track** 1470mm (57.9in) **Unladen weight** 1370kg (3020lb) **Gross vehicle weight** 1810kg (3990lb) **Top speed** 160km/h (99.42mph) **0–100km/h** (0-62mph) 15sec

W128 cabriolets and coupés: 220SE (1958–60) As for contemporary W128 220SE saloon, except: **Engine** Type M127 in-line six-cylinder **Crankshaft** Four main bearings **Bore × stroke** 80mm × 72.8mm **Capacity** 2195cc **Valves** Overhead camshaft **Compression ratio** 8.7:1 **Fuel system** Bosch fuel injection, with twin-piston pump **Maximum power** 115PS at 4800rpm (1958-59), 120PS at 4800rpm (1959-60) **Maximum torque** 19mkg (152lb ft) at 4100rpm **Length** 4670mm (183.9in) **Wheelbase** 2700mm (106.3in) **Width** 1765mm (69.5in) **Height** 1530mm (60.2in) **Unladen weight** 1430kg (3152lb), Coupé; 1470kg (3240lb), Cabriolet **Gross vehicle weight** 1815kg (4001lb) **Top speed** 160km/h (99.42mph) **0–100km/h** (0-62mph) 15sec

W110 190 (1961–65) Engine Type M121 B IV in-line four-cylinder petrol **Crankshaft** Three main bearings **Bore × stroke** 85mm × 83.6mm **Capacity** 1897cc **Valves** Pushrod-operated overhead valves **Compression ratio** 8.7:1 **Fuel system** Solex 34 PJCB carburettor **Maximum power** 80PS at 5000rpm **Maximum torque** 14.5mkg (105lb ft) at 2500rpm **Transmission** Four-speed all-synchromesh gearbox; ratios 4.05:1, 2.28:1, 1.53:1, 1.00:1, reverse 4.05:1. Optional from Aug 1962: four-speed automatic gearbox; ratios 3.98:1, 2.52:1, 1.58:1, 1.00:1, reverse 4.15:1 **Final drive** 4.08:1 **Brakes** Hydraulic drum front and rear, with optional servo assistance; mechanical handbrake on rear wheels. From Aug 1963: dual hydraulic circuit and disc front with servo assistance **Front suspension** Independent, with unequal-length wishbones, coil springs and anti-roll bar **Rear suspension** Single-joint, low-pivot swing-axles, with coil springs and compensating spring; air suspension on rear axle optional from summer 1963 **Steering** Recirculating ball, with 21.4:1 ratio; power-assisted option with 17.3:1 ratio, from May 1964 **Wheels and tyres** 13in wheels with 7.00-13 tyres **Length** 4730mm (186.5in) **Wheelbase** 2700mm (106.3in) **Width** 1795mm (70.7in) **Height** 1495mm (58.8in) **Front track** 1468mm (58in), 1461-63; 1482mm (58.3in), 1963-65 **Rear track** 1485mm (58.5in) **Unladen weight** 1280kg (2822lb), automatic 1320kg (2910lb) **Gross vehicle weight** 1750kg (3858lb) **Top speed** 150km/h (93.2mph), 145km/h (90.1mph) automatic **0–100km/h** (0-62mph) 18sec, automatic 22sec

W110: 190D (1961–65) As for contemporary petrol-engined 190, except: **Engine** Type OM621 III in-line four-cylinder indirect-injection diesel **Crankshaft** Three main bearings **Bore × stroke** 87mm × 83.6mm **Capacity** 1988cc **Valves** Pushrod-operated overhead valves **Compression ratio** 21:1 **Fuel system** Bosch injection pump **Maximum power** 55PS at 4200rpm **Maximum torque** 11.5mkg (86lb ft) at 2400rpm **Final drive** 3.92:1 **Unladen weight** 1320kg (2910lb), automatic 1360kg (2998lb) **Top speed** 130km/h (80.78mph), automatic 127km/h (78.9mph) **0–100km/h** (0-62mph) 29sec, automatic 30sec

W110: 200 (1965–68), 200 Universal (1966–67) As for late 190 petrol models, except: **Engine** Type M121 B XI in-line four-cylinder petrol **Crankshaft** Five main bearings **Bore × stroke** 87mm × 83.6mm **Capacity** 1988cc **Valves** Overhead camshaft **Compression ratio** 9:1 **Fuel system** Two Solex 38 PDSJ carburettors **Maximum power** 95PS at 5200rpm **Maximum torque** 15.7mkg (113.5lb ft) at 3600rpm **Transmission** Four-speed all-synchromesh gearbox; ratios 4.09:1, 2.25:1, 1.42:1, 1.00:1. Optional four-speed automatic on saloon models only; ratios 3.98:1, 2.52:1, 1.58:1, 1.00:1 **Final drive** 4.08:1 **Rear suspension** Air suspension option replaced by hydropneumatic self-levelling option; self-levelling standard on Universal models **Steering** Recirculating ball, with 22.7:1 ratio; optional power-assisted steering with 17.3:1 ratio **Wheels and tyres** 15in wheels with 7.00-15 tyres on Universal models **Length** 4740mm (186.9in), Universal **Wheelbase** 131.8in, Long-wheelbase **Height** 1530mm (60.2 in), Universal **Unladen weight** 1310kg (2888lb), automatic 1350kg (2976lb), Universal 1415kg (3119lb) **Gross vehicle weight** 1775kg (3913lb), Universal 2105kg (4640lb) **Top speed** 161km/h (100mph), automatic 158km/h (98.18mph) **0–100km/h** (0-62mph) 15sec, automatic and Universal 16sec

W110: 200D (1965–68), 200D Universal (1966–67), 200D seven-seater (1967–68) As for contemporary 200 petrol models, except: **Engine** Type OM621 VIII in-line four-cylinder indirect-injection diesel **Crankshaft** Five main bearings **Bore × stroke** 87mm × 83.6mm **Capacity** 1988cc **Valves** Overhead camshaft **Compression ratio** 21:1 **Fuel system** Bosch injection pump **Maximum power** 55PS at 4200rpm **Maximum torque** 11.5mkg (83lb ft) at 2400rpm **Transmission** No automatic option for Universal or seven-seater models **Final drive** 3.92:1, 4.08:1 Universal and seven-seater **Unladen weight** 1350kg (2976lb), automatic 1390kg (3064lb), Universal 1455kg (3208lb), seven-seater 1490kg (3285lb) **Gross vehicle weight** 1825kg (4023lb), seven-seater 2110kg (4652lb), Universal 2155kg (4751lb) **Top speed** 130km/h (80.78mph), automatic 127km/h (78.92mph), seven-seater 125km/h (77.67mph) **0–100km/h** (0-62mph) 29sec, automatic 30sec, Universal and seven-seater n/a

W110: 230 (1965–68), 230 Universal (1966–67) As for W110 200 models, except: **Engine** Type M180 VI in-line six-cylinder petrol (1965-66), type M180 VIII in-line six-cylinder petrol (1966-68) **Crankshaft** Seven main bearings **Bore × stroke** 82mm × 72.8mm **Capacity** 2281cc **Valves** Overhead camshaft **Compression ratio** 9:1 **Fuel system** Two Solex 38 PDSI-2 carburettors (1965-66), two Zenith 35/40 INAT carburettors (1966-68) **Maximum power** 105PS at 5200rpm (1965-66), 120PS at 5400rpm (1966-68) **Maximum torque** 17.7mkg (128lb ft) at 3600rpm (1965-66), 18.2mkg (132lb ft) at 4000rpm (1966-68) **Rear suspension** Optional hydropneumatic self-levelling; self-levelling standard on Universal models **Unladen weight** 1350kg (2976lb), automatic 1390kg (3064lb) **Gross vehicle weight** 1805kg (3979lb) **Top speed** 168km/h (104.39mph), 1965-66; 165km/h (102.53mph), automatic 1965-66; 175km/h (108.74mph), 1966-68; 172km/h (106.88mph), automatic 1966-68 **0–100km/h** (0-62mph) 14sec, 1965-66; 16sec, automatic, 1965-66; 13sec, 1966-68; 15sec, automatic, 1966-68

W111 saloon models: 220 (1959–65), 220S (1959–65) **Engine** Type M180 IV in-line six-cylinder petrol **Crankshaft** Four main bearings **Bore × stroke** 80mm × 72.8mm **Capacity** 2195cc **Valves** Overhead camshaft **Compression ratio** 8.7:1 **Fuel system** Two Solex 34 PJCB carburettors (220), two Solex 34 PAJTA carburettors (220S, 1959-63), two Solex 35/40 INAT carburettors with automatic choke (220S, 1963-65) **Maximum power** 95PS at 4800rpm (220), 100PS at 5000rpm (220S) **Maximum torque** 17.2mkg (124lb ft) at 3200rpm (220), 17.5mkg (127lb ft) at 3500rpm (220S) **Transmission** Four-speed all-synchromesh gearbox; ratios 3.64:1, 2.36:1 (2.28:1 from 1962), 1.53:1, 1.00:1, reverse 3.92:1. Four-speed automatic optional from 1962; ratios 3.98:1, 2.52:1, 1.58:1, 1.00:1 **Final drive** 3.90:1 optional (220), 4.10:1 (220S) **Brakes** Hydraulic drum front and rear

with optional servo assistance; mechanical handbrake on rear wheels (220). From Aug 1963: dual hydraulic circuit and disc front with servo assistance (220); hydraulic drum front and rear with servo assistance, mechanical handbrake on rear wheels (220S). From Apr 1962: disc front (220S). From Aug 1963: dual hydraulic circuit (220S) **Front suspension** Independent, with unequal-length wishbones, coil springs and anti-roll bar **Rear suspension** Single-joint, low-pivot swing-axles, with coil springs and compensating spring; air suspension option on rear axle from summer 1963 **Steering** Recirculating ball, with 21.4:1 ratio; optional power-assisted type with 17.3:1 ratio **Wheels and tyres** 13in wheels with 6.70-13 tyres (1959-60) or 7.25-13 tyres (1960-65) **Length** 4875mm (191.9in) **Wheelbase** 2750mm (108.3in) **Width** 1795mm (70.7in) **Height** 1500mm (59.1in) **Front track** 1470mm (57.9in), 1959-63; 1482mm (58.3in), 1963-65 **Rear track** 1485mm (58.5in) **Unladen weight** 1320kg (2910lb), 220; 1360kg (2998lb), 220 automatic; 1350kg (2976lb), 220S; 1390kg (3064lb), 220S automatic **Gross vehicle weight** 1760kg (3880lb), 220, 1959-60; 1820kg (4012lb), 220, 1960-65; 1780kg (3924lb), 220S, 1959-60; 1845kg (4067lb), 220S, 1960-65 **Top speed** 160km/h (99.42mph), 220; 165km/h (102.52mph), 220S **0-100km/h** (0-62mph) 16sec (220), 15sec (220S)

W111 saloon models: 220SE (1959-65) As for W111 220S models, except: **Engine** Type M127 III in-line six-cylinder petrol **Crankshaft** Four main bearings **Bore × stroke** 80mm × 72.8mm **Capacity** 2195cc **Valves** Overhead camshaft **Compression ratio** 8.7:1 **Fuel system** Bosch mechanical fuel injection **Maximum power** 120PS at 4800rpm **Maximum torque** 19.3mkg (140lb ft) at 3900rpm **Unladen weight** 1380kg (3042lb); 1420kg (3130lb), automatic **Gross vehicle weight** 1810kg (3990lb), 1959-60; 1875kg (4133lb), 1960-65 **Top speed** 172km/h (106.87mph) **0-100km/h** (0-62mph) 14sec **Typical fuel consumption** 14 litres/100km (16.77mpg), automatic 15 litres/100km (15.65mpg)

W111 saloon models: 230S (1965-68), 230S Universal (1966-67) As for W111 220 saloons, except: **Engine** Type M180 VIII in-line six-cylinder petrol **Crankshaft** Seven main bearings **Bore × stroke** 82mm × 72.8mm **Capacity** 2281cc **Valves** Overhead camshaft **Compression ratio** 9:1 **Fuel system** Two Zenith 35/40 INAT carburettors **Maximum power** 120PS at 5400rpm **Maximum torque** 18.2mkg (132lb ft) at 4000rpm **Transmission** Four-speed all-synchromesh gearbox; ratios 4.05:1, 2.23:1, 1.42:1, 1.00:1. Optional four-speed automatic gearbox; ratios 3.98:1, 2.52:1, 1.58:1, 1.00:1 **Final drive** 4.08:1 **Brakes** Hydraulic with dual circuit and servo assistance; discs at front and drums at rear; mechanical handbrake on rear wheels **Rear suspension** With hydropneumatic self-levelling **Steering** Recirculating ball, with 22.7:1 ratio; optional power-assisted type with 17.3:1 ratio **Wheels and tyres** 15in wheels with 7.00-15 tyres (Universal models) **Length** 4885mm (192.3in), Universal **Height** 1500mm (58.8in), saloon; 1530mm (60.2in), Universal **Unladen weight** 1410kg (3108lb); 1450kg (3197lb), automatic; 1510kg (3329lb), Universal; 1550kg (3417lb), Universal automatic **Gross vehicle weight** 1850kg (4078lb); 2170kg (4784lb), Universal **Top speed** 176km/h (109.36mph); 174km/h (108.12mph), automatic **0-100km/h** (0-62mph) 13sec, 15sec automatic

W111 cabriolets and coupés: 220SE (1961-65) Engine Type M127 III in-line six-cylinder petrol **Crankshaft** Four main bearings **Bore × stroke** 80mm × 72.8mm **Capacity** 2195cc **Valves** Overhead camshaft **Compression ratio** 8.7:1 **Fuel system** Bosch mechanical fuel injection **Maximum power** 120PS at 4800rpm **Maximum torque** 19.3mkg (140lb ft) at 3900rpm **Transmission** Four-speed all-synchromesh gearbox; ratios 3.64:1, 2.36:1 (2.28:1 from 1962), 1.53:1, 1.00:1, reverse 3.92:1. Four-speed automatic optional; ratios 3.98:1, 2.52:1, 1.58:1, 1.00:1 **Final drive** 4.10:1 **Brakes** Hydraulic with servo assistance; discs at front and drums at rear; mechanical handbrake on rear wheels. From Aug 1963: dual hydraulic circuit **Front suspension** Independent, with unequal-length wishbones, coil springs and anti-roll

bar **Rear suspension** Single-joint, low-pivot swing-axles, with coil springs and compensating spring; air suspension option on the rear axle from summer 1963 **Steering** Recirculating ball, with 22.7:1 ratio; optional power-assisted type with 17.3:1 ratio **Wheels and tyres** 13in wheels with 7.25-13 tyres (coupé) or 7.50-13 tyres (cabriolet) **Length** 4880mm (192.1in) **Wheelbase** 2750mm (108.3in) **Width** 1845mm (72.7in) **Height** 1445mm (57in) **Front track** 1482mm (58.3in) **Rear track** 1485mm (58.5in) **Unladen weight** 1450kg (3197lb), Coupé; 1490kg (3285lb), Coupé automatic; 1520kg (3351lb), Cabriolet; 1560kg (3439lb), Cabriolet automatic **Gross vehicle weight** 1880kg (4145lb), Coupé; 1950kg (4299lb), Cabriolet **Top speed** 172km/h (106.87mph) **0-100km/h** (0-62mph) 14sec

W111 cabriolets and coupés: 250SE (1965-67) Engine Type M129 in-line six-cylinder petrol **Crankshaft** Seven main bearings **Bore × stroke** 82mm × 78.8mm **Capacity** 2496cc **Valves** Overhead camshaft **Compression ratio** 9.3:1 **Fuel system** Bosch mechanical fuel injection with six-piston pump **Maximum power** 150PS at 5500rpm **Maximum torque** 22mkg (159lb ft) at 4200rpm **Transmission** Four-speed all-synchromesh gearbox; ratios 4.05:1, 2.23:1, 1.42:1, 1.00:1, reverse 3.92:1. Four-speed automatic optional; ratios 3.98:1, 2.52:1, 1.58:1, 1.00:1 **Final drive** 3.92:1 **Brakes** Hydraulic with dual circuit and servo assistance; discs at front and drums at rear; mechanical handbrake on rear wheels **Front suspension** Independent, with unequal-length wishbones, coil springs and anti-roll bar **Rear suspension** Single-joint, low-pivot swing-axles, with coil springs and compensating spring; hydropneumatic self-levelling **Steering** Recirculating ball, with 22.7:1 ratio; optional power-assisted type with 17.3:1 ratio **Wheels and tyres** 14in wheels with 7.35-14 or 185-14 tyres (coupé); 14in wheels with 7.75-14 or 195/14 tyres (cabriolet) **Length** 4880mm (192.1in) **Wheelbase** 2750mm (108.3in) **Width** 1845mm (72.7in) **Height** 1420mm (55.9in), Coupé; 1435mm (56.5in), Cabriolet **Front track** 1482mm (58.3in) **Rear track** 1485mm (58.5in) **Unladen weight** 1490kg (3285lb), Coupé; 1530kg (3373lb), Coupé automatic; 1575kg (3472lb), Cabriolet; 1615kg (3560lb), Cabriolet automatic **Gross vehicle weight** 1960kg (4321lb), Coupé; 2045kg (4508lb), Cabriolet **Top speed** 193km/h (119.92mph); 188km/h (116.82mph), automatic **0-100km/h** (0-62mph) 12sec

W112 saloon models: 300SE (1961-65), 300SE Long-wheelbase (1963-65) Engine Type M189 in-line six-cylinder petrol **Crankshaft** Seven main bearings **Bore × stroke** 85mm × 88mm **Capacity** 2996cc **Valves** Overhead camshaft **Compression ratio** 8.7:1 (1961-64), 8.8:1 (1964-65) **Fuel system** Bosch mechanical fuel injection with two-plunger pump (1961-64), Bosch mechanical fuel injection with six-piston pump (1964-65) **Maximum power** 160PS at 5000rpm (1961-64), 170PS at 5400rpm (1964-65) **Maximum torque** 25.6mkg (185lb ft) at 3800rpm (1961-64), 25.4mkg (183lb ft) at 4000rpm (1964-1965) **Transmission** Four-speed all-synchromesh gearbox; ratios 4.05:1, 2.28:1, 1.53:1, 1.00:1, reverse 4.15:1. Optional four-speed automatic gearbox (standard in USA); ratios 3.98:1, 2.52:1, 1.58:1, 1.00:1 **Final drive** 3.92:1 or 3.75:1 (manual gearbox), 4.10:1 (automatic gearbox, 1961-63), 3.92:1 or 3.75:1 (automatic gearbox, 1963-65); limited-slip differential from Mar 1962 **Brakes** Hydraulic dual-circuit with power assistance and discs on all four wheels **Front suspension** Independent, with unequal-length wishbones, air springs and anti-roll bar **Rear suspension** Single-joint, low-pivot swing axles, with air springs incorporating self-levelling, and anti-roll bar **Steering** Power-assisted, with 17.3:1 ratio **Wheels and tyres** 13in wheels with 7.50-13 tyres **Length** 4875mm (191.9in), standard saloon; 4975mm (195.8in), long-wheelbase saloon **Wheelbase** 2750mm (108.3in), standard saloon; 2850mm (112.2in), long-wheelbase saloon **Width** 1795mm (70.7in) **Height** 1455mm (58in) **Front track** 1482mm (58.3in) **Rear track** 1490mm (58.6in) **Unladen weight** 1580kg (3483lb); 1620kg (3571lb), automatic; 1630kg (3593lb), long-wheelbase; 1670kg (3682lb), long-wheelbase automatic **Gross vehicle weight** 2065kg (4552lb); 2115kg (4663lb), long-wheelbase **Top speed** 1961-

64: 180km/h (111mph), 3.92 axle; 175km/h (109mph), 3.92 axle automatic. 1965-67: 190km/h (118mph), 3.92 axle; 185km/h (115mph), 3.92 axle automatic; 200km/h (124mph), 3.75 axle; 195km/h (121mph), 3.75 axle automatic **0-100km/h** (0-62mph) 13sec, 1961-64; 12sec, 1965-67

W112 cabriolets and coupés: 300SE (1962-67) As for contemporary W112 saloons, except: **Wheels and tyres** 14in wheels with 7.35-14 or 185/14 tyres (1965-67, Coupé); 14in wheels with 7.75-

14 or 195/14 tyres (1965-67, Cabriolet) **Length** 4880mm (192.1in) **Width** 1845mm (72.7in) **Height** 1400mm (54.9in), Coupé; 1435mm (55.1in), Cabriolet **Unladen weight** 1962-65: 1600kg (3527lb), Coupé; 1640kg (3615lb), Coupé automatic; 1700kg (3748lb), Cabriolet; 1740kg (3836lb), Cabriolet automatic. 1965-67: 1650kg (3637lb), Coupé; 1690kg (3726lb), Coupé automatic; 1715kg (3781lb), Cabriolet; 1755kg (3869lb), Cabriolet automatic **Gross vehicle weight** 1962-65: 2060kg (4541lb), Coupé; 2160kg (4762lb), Cabriolet. 1965-67: 2120kg (4674lb), Coupé; 2185kg (4817lb), Cabriolet

Production figures...

PONTON FOUR-CYLINDER SALOON AND UTILITY MODELS

	180	180a	180b	180c	Total
1953	4362				4362
1954	20306				20306
1955	17704				17704
1956	8464				8464
1957	1350	4656			6006
1958		15967			15967
1959		6730	7314		14044
1960			14384		14384
1961			7717	4980	12697
1962				4300	4300
Total	52186	27353	29415	9280	118234

The rolling chassis built for conversion into utility vehicles such as ambulances are included in the above figures. An annual breakdown is not available, but by model the totals were: 180 279, 180a 198, 180b 382, 180c 183, total 1042.

	180D	180Da	180Db	180Dc	Total
1953	11				11
1954	15532				15532
1955	20345				20345
1956	21013	*			21013
1957	*	22910			22910
1958		26693			26693
1959		9981	8076		18057
1960			11151		11151
1961			5449	4822	10271
1962				7000	7000
Total	56901	59584	24676	11822	152983

* The exact production figures for 180D and 180Da models in 1956 and 1957 are not clear. The totals given here are the annual totals for diesel 180s in those two years, irrespective of model.

The rolling chassis built for conversion into utility vehicles such as ambulances are included in the above figures. An annual breakdown is not available, but by model the totals were: 180D and 180Da 2439, 180Db 400, 180Dc 222, total 3061.

	190	190D	190b	190Db	Total
1956	16001				16001
1957	22578				22578
1958	15791	5469			21260
1959	6975	15160	6613	13709	42457
1960			12986	29116	42102
1961			8864	18464	27328
Total	61345	20629	28463	61309	171746

Total of 190 and 190b: 89,808. Total of 190D and 190Db: 81,938.

The rolling chassis built for conversion into utility vehicles such as ambulances are included in the above figures. An annual breakdown is not available, but by model the totals were: 190 354, 190b 349, total 703. 190D 136, 190Db 711, total 847.

PONTON SIX-CYLINDER SALOON AND UTILITY MODELS

	220	220S	219	220SE	Total
1954	4178				4178
1955	19348				19348
1956	2411	10525	5474		18410
1957		15469	8505		23974
1958		20181	9296	201	29678
1959		9114	4570	1773	15457
Total	25937	55279	27845	1974	111045

The rolling chassis built for conversion into utility vehicles such as ambulances are included in the above figures. An annual breakdown is not available, but by model the totals were: 219 3, 220S 11, total 14. There were no 220 or 220SE rolling chassis.

PONTON CABRIOLETS AND COUPÉS

	220S	220SE	Total
1956	297		297
1957	1066		1066
1958	1280	114	1394
1959	786	628	1414
1960		1200	1200
Total	3429	1942	5371

An annual breakdown into cabriolet and coupé models built is not available, but by model the totals were: 220S 2178 cabriolets & 1251 coupés, 220SE 1112 cabriolets & 830 coupés, total 3290 cabriolets & 2081 coupés.

PONTON MODELS, OVERALL TOTALS

	Four-cyl	Six-cyl	Total
1953	4373		4373
1954	35838	4178	40016
1955	38049	19348	57397
1956	45478	18707	64185
1957	51494	25030	76524
1958	63920	31072	94992
1959	74558	16871	91429
1960	67637	1200	68837
1961	50316		50316
1962	11300		11300
Total	442963	116406	559369

FINTAIL FOUR-CYLINDER SALOON AND UTILITY MODELS

	190	190D	200	200D	Total
1961	9249	12882			22131
1962	31275	45414			76689
1963	35457	60784			96241
1964	33776	64422			98198
1965	20797	42143	16864	30937	110741
1966			26842	61707	88549
1967			26169	68399	94568
1968			332	575	907
Total	130554	225645	70207	161618	588024

Figures for the four-cylinder rolling chassis supplied for special bodywork are not available. There were ambulances and their Kombi (estate car) derivatives by Miesen and Binz on 190 and 190D rolling chassis from 1962, and on 200 and 200D rolling chassis from 1965. In 1966-67, there were Universal estate cars by IMA on the 200 and 200D rolling chassis, and in 1967-68 there were long-wheelbase seven-seater derivatives of the 200D. Production figures for all these models are included in the totals given above.

FINTAIL SIX-CYLINDER SALOON AND ESTATE MODELS

	220	220S	220SE	230	230S	300SE	300SE (LWB)	Total
1959	3375	7267	1579					12221
1960	13127	26642	9247					49016
1961	14842	32238	10761			13		57854
1962	11618	26077	10786			2768	1	51250
1963	10492	26236	12648			995	387	50758
1964	11327	28732	14336			936	751	56082
1965	4910	13927	6529	8548	12621	490	407	47432
1966				14951	17320			32271
1967				16441	11176			27617
1968				318	80			398
Total	69691	161119	65886	40258	41197	5202	1546	384899

No six-cylinder Fintail rolling chassis were supplied for utility bodywork. However, in 1966-67, 230 and 230S rolling chassis were converted into Kombis (estate cars) by IMA. Figures for these conversions are not available, and the vehicles are included in the totals given above. The overall production total of Fintail saloons and derivatives (excluding the cabriolets and coupés) was 972,923.

FINTAIL CABRIOLET AND COUPÉ MODELS

	220SE	250SE	300SE	Total
1960	2			2
1961	2537			2537
1962	4287		331	4618
1963	3755		630	4385
1964	3528		706	4234
1965	2793	1205	710	4708
1966		3601	497	4098
1967		1407	253	1660
Total	16902	6213	3127	26242

It is not possible to divide the totals above into individual figures for coupé and cabriolet models.

In later years, there were further derivatives of these cars, as follows: 280SE (1967-71) 5187, 280SE 3.5 (1969-71) 4502.

Identification by chassis numbers

Two different vehicle numbering systems were used on the cars covered in this book, as follows.

1953-59
The numbers have 14 digits on LHD cars and 15 digits on RHD cars.
First digit: R (RHD models only; LHD cars have no prefix)
Next three digits: type (as W number)
Next three digits: body type
Eighth digit: N (standard transmission) or Z (Hydrak clutch)
Next two digits: production year in reverse (eg, 85 = 1958, etc)
Last five digits: serial number

1960 onwards
The numbers have 14 digits on all models.
First three digits: type (as W number)
Next three digits: body type
Seventh digit: 1 (LHD) or 2 (RHD)
Eighth digit: 0 (standard transmission), 1 (Hydrak clutch) or 2 (automatic)
Last six digits: serial number

PONTON FOUR-CYLINDER SALOON AND UTILITY MODELS

	180	180D	190	190D
Saloon	120.010	120.110	121.010	121.110
Saloon with sunroof	-	-	121.011	121.111
Ambulance	120.000	120.100	121.000	121.100
Special body, 2-door	120.001	120.101	-	-
Special body, 4-door	120.002	120.102	-	-
Special body	-	-	121.002	121.102

PONTON SIX-CYLINDER SALOON AND UTILITY MODELS

	219	220	220S	220SE
Saloon	105.010	180.010	180.010	128.010
Saloon with sunroof	105.011	180.011	180.011	128.011
Ambulance	105.000	180.000	180.000	-

PONTON CABRIOLET AND COUPÉ MODELS

	220S	220SE
Cabriolet	180.030	128.030
Coupé	180.037	128.037

FINTAIL FOUR-CYLINDER SALOON AND UTILITY MODELS

	190	190D	200	200D
Saloon	110.010	110.110	110.010	110.110
Ambulance	110.000	110.100	110.000	110.100
Special body	110.001	110.101	110.001	110.101
LWB Ambulance	-	-	110.004	-
LWB Taxi	-	-	110.016	-

FINTAIL SIX-CYLINDER SALOON AND ESTATE MODELS

	220	220S	220SE
Saloon	111.010	111.012	111.014
Ambulance	111.000	-	-
Special body	111.001	-	-

	230	230S	300SE
Saloon	110.010	111.012	112.014
Saloon, long-wheelbase	-	-	112.105
Ambulance	110.002	111.000	-
Special body	110.003	111.001	-
LWB Ambulance	110.005	-	-
LWB Taxi	110.017	-	-

FINTAIL CABRIOLET AND COUPÉ MODELS

	220SE	250SE	300SE
Cabriolet	111.021	111.021	112.021
Coupé	111.023	111.023	112.023

ACKNOWLEDGEMENTS

Most of the colour photographs in this book were provided by
Dieter Rebmann (Germany) and Dennis Adler (USA), although
their work was supplemented by shots from James Mann (UK) of a
250SE kindly loaned by The Garage on the Green, Fulham, London
(0171 384 1100). Thanks must also go to Dieter Ritter of the
Mercedes-Benz Museum for permitting photography of cars from
the company's collection. The main source of period photographs
was the Daimler-Benz Classic Archiv in Stuttgart, where the help of
Dr Harry Niemann and Fred Langer is acknowledged. As well as
doing the picture research in Stuttgart, Nick Kisch kindly loaned
many pictures from his own collection. Other photographs have
come from Haymarket Publishing Ltd and the collections of James
Taylor and David Hodges.

**A selection of six-cylinder Fintail models lines up in South Africa
during the early 1960s, with a 220SE cabriolet in the foreground.**